W9-BVR-404

Other atlases in the PLUTO PROJECTS series:

THE NEW STATE OF THE WORLD ATLAS
by Michael Kidron and Ronald Segal
4th edition 1991

THE STATE OF THE EARTH ATLAS
by Joni Seager
2nd edition (forthcoming) 1994

THE NEW STATE OF WAR AND PEACE
by Michael Kidron and Dan Smith
2nd edition 1991

THE STATE OF HEALTH ATLAS
by Judith Mackay
1st edition 1993

THE STATE OF THE UNITED STATES
by Doug Henwood
1st edition (forthcoming) 1994

THE STATE OF RELIGION ATLAS

THE
STATE OF RELIGION
ATLAS

Joanne O'Brien and Martin Palmer
Consultant Editor: David B. Barrett

A PLUTO PROJECT

A TOUCHSTONE BOOK
Published by Simon & Schuster

New York   London   Toronto   Sydney   Tokyo   Singapore

TOUCHSTONE
Simon & Schuster Building
Rockefeller Center
1230 Avenue of the Americas
New York, New York 10021

Published in Great Britain by
Simon & Schuster Ltd., London

Edited and coordinated for Myriad Editions by Anne Benewick
with Candida Lacey

Maps created by Swanston Graphics Limited, Derby, England
Artwork and design by Isabelle Lewis
with Andrew Bright and Jeanne Radford

Additional design by Corinne Pearlman

Printed and bound in Hong Kong
Produced by Mandarin Offset Ltd.

10 9 8 7 6 5 4 3 2 1 ppb

Library of Congress Cataloging-in-Publication Data
available on request

ISBN 0-671-79376-4

CONTENTS

INTRODUCTION

Medieval theologians are reputed to have tried to work out how many angels could dance on the head of a pin. A data-based assessment of the worldwide state of religion today has at times felt like a similar task!

This atlas shows at a glance the major contours of the religious world, as summed up within the formal structures of the major faiths and the relationships between them. The maps also highlight effectively the position of the major faiths in relation to important contemporary issues such as the environment and the status of women. In working on this unique project, we have all been conscious of both its strengths and weaknesses. Given the sheer diversity of worldwide religious belief we have found it necessary to give more emphasis to the major faiths than is perhaps justified. There are hints of this wider diversity in map 9. Traditional Beliefs, and map 10. New Religious Movements, but inevitably, with maps conceived on a global scale and in limited space, the local and unquantifiable has often had to be lost.

This atlas deals primarily, therefore, with the worlds of Buddhism, Christianity, Hinduism, Islam, Judaism, Sikhism and traditional beliefs as a group, including Chinese popular religion. In deciding on what issues to cover in the maps, we were obviously constrained by those which could be illustrated and on which we could offer substantial and reliable evidence. However, not all religious organizations consider the production of regular, statistical annual reports as being an essential part of their faith! To find appropriate subjects with sufficient data, we have sifted through materials from around the world, benefitting in the process from the unrivalled database of David B. Barrett.

Many of these maps represent the fullest and most up-to-date information available, as in the maps on popular religions (map 1) and on the Christian missionary movement (map 14). In other maps, on Christian and Muslim giving, for example (maps 17 and 18), we have merely tried to give a feel for a vast area and identified particular aid agencies to show the spread of such work worldwide. In some maps we have tried to focus on wider phenomena, as in the map on holy cities (map 33). And yet others illustrate ideas that are currently much-debated and even highly controversial, such as female deities (map 12), Islamic banking (map 19) and the future of the major faiths (map 31).

The pictures which emerge of the state of religion are quite stark. The maps give substance to issues and developments in ways which may be unexpected: on the continued rise of Christianity and Islam and the consequential demise of traditional religions; on the re-emergence of religion, following the collapse of Communism, and the consequent tendency to diversification; on the extent of formal ties between individual religions and states; and on the scale of religious involvement in warfare.

This is the first attempt to convey worldwide religious diversity in maps of this kind. While we have sought to find and use all relevant data, there are surely many sources which have remained untapped by us. The next edition, we hope, will not only be more up-to-date, but will tackle topics for which, this time round, available data was simply inadequate. The wealth of the major faiths is but one example of a topic we would like to have covered, but we could neither find relevant data nor agree on appropriate criteria. If you have information which may contribute to, refute, or expand a topic dealt with here, do please let us know, citing your source.

As authors, we have relied heavily upon friends and colleagues from the different faiths, all of whom are acknowledged, either on the maps themselves or in the notes to the maps at the back of the atlas. The most invaluable aid has been offered by our consultant editor, David B. Barrett, a mine of information, without whose pioneer work we could never have considered undertaking this task. Our thanks also to all our colleagues in the International Consultancy on Religion, Education and Culture (ICOREC). Finally, our thanks to our editor, Anne Benewick, whose vision this atlas originally was and whose tireless work has helped us on our way.

Joanne O'Brien
Martin Palmer
Manchester, June 1993

Part 1

PRESENT AND PAST
BELIEFS

Copyright © Myriad Editions Limited

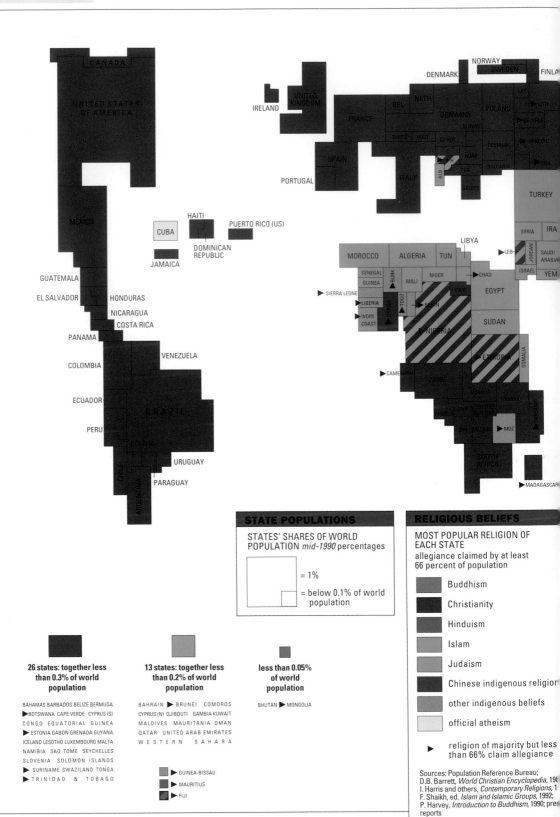

STATE POPULATIONS

STATES' SHARES OF WORLD
POPULATION *mid-1990* percentages

☐ = 1%

▫ = below 0.1% of world
population

RELIGIOUS BELIEFS

MOST POPULAR RELIGION OF
EACH STATE
allegiance claimed by at least
66 percent of population

Buddhism

Christianity

Hinduism

Islam

Judaism

Chinese indigenous religion

other indigenous beliefs

official atheism

► religion of majority but less
than 66% claim allegiance

Sources: Population Reference Bureau;
D.B. Barrett, *World Christian Encyclopedia*, 198[
I. Harris and others, *Contemporary Religions*, 1
F. Shaikh, ed. *Islam and Islamic Groups*, 1992;
P. Harvey, *Introduction to Buddhism*, 1990; pres
reports

**26 states: together less
than 0.3% of world
population**

BAHAMAS BARBADOS BELIZE BERMUDA
►BOTSWANA CAPE VERDE CYPRUS (S)
CONGO EQUATORIAL GUINEA
►ESTONIA GABON GRENADA GUYANA
ICELAND LESOTHO LUXEMBOURG MALTA
NAMIBIA SAO TOME SEYCHELLES
SLOVENIA SOLOMON ISLANDS
► SURINAME SWAZILAND TONGA
►TRINIDAD & TOBAGO

**13 states: together less
than 0.2% of world
population**

BAHRAIN ► BRUNEI COMOROS
CYPRUS (N) DJIBOUTI GAMBIA KUWAIT
MALDIVES MAURITANIA OMAN
QATAR UNITED ARAB EMIRATES
WESTERN SAHARA

GUINEA-BISSAU
MAURITIUS
► FIJI

**less than 0.05%
of world
population**

BHUTAN ► MONGOLIA

In more than 80 percent of the world's states at least two thirds of the population claim allegiance to a single faith. For Christians in Europe this is no indication of regular church attendance.

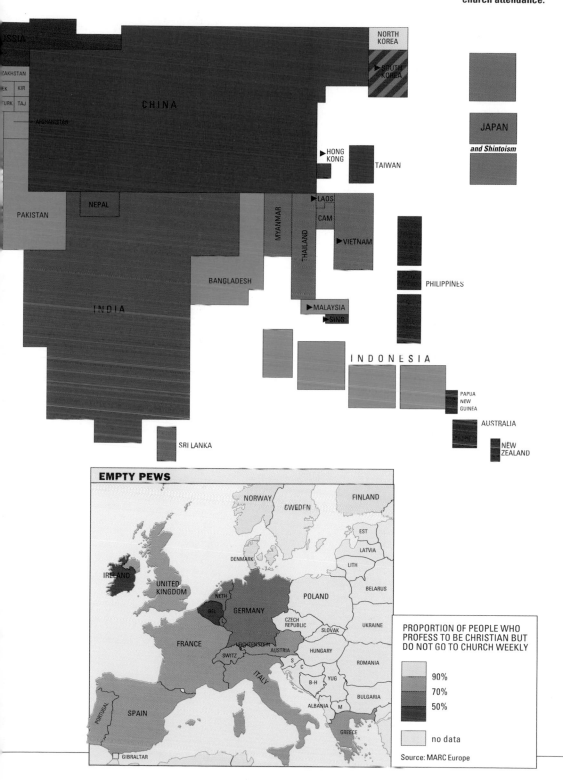

RUSSIA

KAZAKHSTAN

EX | KIR
TURK | TAJ

AFGHANISTAN

CHINA

NORTH KOREA

▶ SOUTH KOREA

JAPAN

and Shintoism

PAKISTAN

NEPAL

▶ HONG KONG

TAIWAN

MYANMAR

THAILAND

▶ LAOS

CAM

▶ VIETNAM

PHILIPPINES

INDIA

BANGLADESH

▶ MALAYSIA

▶ SING

INDONESIA

PAPUA NEW GUINEA

SRI LANKA

AUSTRALIA

NEW ZEALAND

EMPTY PEWS

NORWAY

SWEDEN

FINLAND

EST

LATVIA

LITH

DENMARK

IRELAND

UNITED KINGDOM

NETH

BEL

GERMANY

POLAND

BELARUS

CZECH REPUBLIC

SLOVAK

UKRAINE

LEICHTENSTEIN

AUSTRIA

HUNGARY

SWITZ

FRANCE

S

C

ITALY

B-H

YUG

ROMANIA

BULGARIA

ALBANIA

M

PORTUGAL

SPAIN

GREECE

GIBRALTAR

PROPORTION OF PEOPLE WHO PROFESS TO BE CHRISTIAN BUT DO NOT GO TO CHURCH WEEKLY

90%
70%
50%

no data

Source: MARC Europe

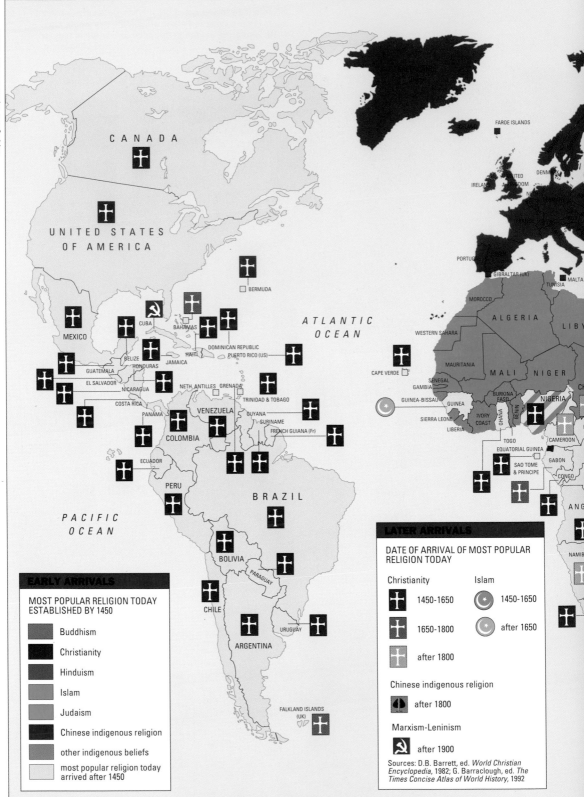

CANADA

UNITED STATES
OF AMERICA

BERMUDA

MEXICO

CUBA
BAHAMAS

BELIZE
HONDURAS
GUATEMALA
EL SALVADOR
NICARAGUA
COSTA RICA
PANAMA

HAITI
JAMAICA
DOMINICAN REPUBLIC
PUERTO RICO (US)

NETH. ANTILLES GRENADA

TRINIDAD & TOBAGO

VENEZUELA

GUYANA
SURINAME
FRENCH GUIANA (Fr)

COLOMBIA

ECUADOR

PERU

BRAZIL

BOLIVIA

PARAGUAY

CHILE

URUGUAY

ARGENTINA

ATLANTIC
OCEAN

PACIFIC
OCEAN

FALKLAND ISLANDS
(UK)

FAROE ISLANDS

IRELAND
UNITED
KINGDOM
DENMARK
NETH...
FRANCE...

PORTUGAL
GIBRALTAR (UK)
TUNISIA
MALTA

MOROCCO

WESTERN SAHARA

ALGERIA

LIBY...

MAURITANIA

MALI

NIGER

CAPE VERDE

SENEGAL
GAMBIA
GUINEA-BISSAU
GUINEA
SIERRA LEONE
LIBERIA

BURKINA
FASO

IVORY
COAST

GHANA

TOGO
BENIN

NIGERIA

CH...

CAMEROON

EQUATORIAL GUINEA
SAO TOME
& PRINCIPE

GABON

CONGO

ANG...

NAMIB...

EARLY ARRIVALS

MOST POPULAR RELIGION TODAY
ESTABLISHED BY 1450

- Buddhism
- Christianity
- Hinduism
- Islam
- Judaism
- Chinese indigenous religion
- other indigenous beliefs
- most popular religion today
  arrived after 1450

LATER ARRIVALS

DATE OF ARRIVAL OF MOST POPULAR
RELIGION TODAY

Christianity
- 1450-1650
- 1650-1800
- after 1800

Islam
- 1450-1650
- after 1650

Chinese indigenous religion
- after 1800

Marxism-Leninism
- after 1900

Sources: D.B. Barrett, ed. *World Christian
Encyclopedia*, 1982; G. Barraclough, ed. *The
Times Concise Atlas of World History*, 1992

18

Over the last 500 years, Christianity has gained more new followers than any other religion, usually replacing local indigenous religions.

Brazil Brunei
Burundi Cameroon
Canada Central African Republic
Chile Colombia Congo Costa Rica
Dominican Republic Ecuador El Salvador
Equatorial Guinea Fiji Gabon Gambia Ghana
Grenada Guatemala Guinea Guyana Haiti Honduras
Indonesia Jamaica Kenya Lesotho Madagascar Malawi
Malaysia Mali Mauritius Mexico Namibia New Caledonia
New Zealand Nicaragua Nigeria Panama Papua New Guinea
Paraguay Peru Philippines Rwanda Senegal Seychelles
South Africa Suriname Swaziland Tanzania Tonga
Trinidad & Tobago Uganda USA Uruguay

Angola Argentina Australia Bahamas Barbados Belize Bermuda Bolivia Botswana

Venezuela Zaire Zambia Zimbabwe

FALLEN LEAVES

STATES IN WHICH INDIGENOUS BELIEFS, THE RELIGION OF THE MAJORITY IN 1450, HAVE NOW BEEN SUPERSEDED

Sources: D.B. Barrett, ed. *World Christian Encyclopedia*, 1982; G. Barraclough, ed. *The Times Concise Atlas of World History*, 1992

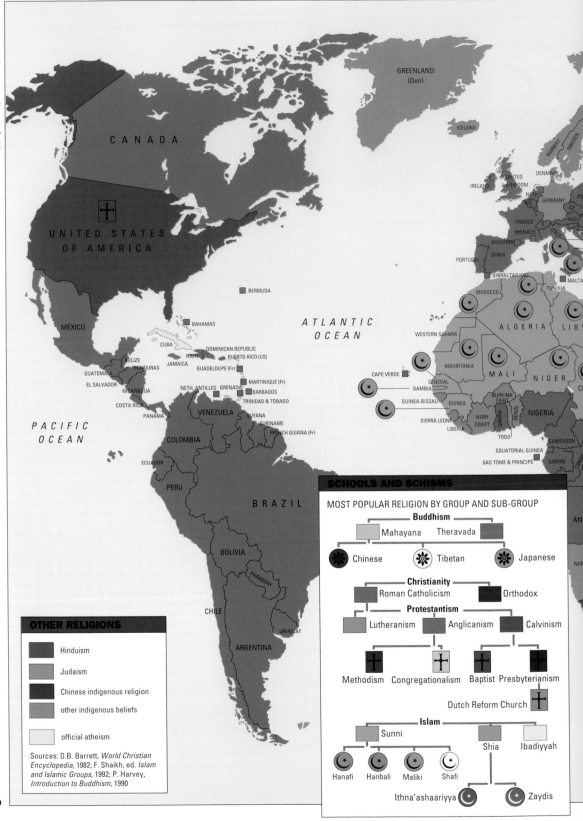

GREENLAND
(Den)

ICELAND

NORWAY
SWEDEN

CANADA

DENMARK

IRELAND
UNITED
KINGDOM
NETH.
BEL.
GERMANY
POL.

UNITED STATES
OF AMERICA

FRANCE
MONACO
CZ
AUS.
SWITZ
ITALY

ANDORRA
SPAIN

PORTUGAL

GIBRALTAR (UK)
MALTA

BERMUDA

MOROCCO
TUNISIA

ATLANTIC
OCEAN

WESTERN SAHARA
ALGERIA
LIBYA

BAHAMAS

MEXICO

CUBA

DOMINICAN REPUBLIC
HAITI
PUERTO RICO (US)

BELIZE
JAMAICA
GUADELOUPE (Fr)

GUATEMALA
HONDURAS

EL SALVADOR

NICARAGUA

MARTINIQUE (Fr)

NETH. ANTILLES
GRENADA
BARBADOS

COSTA RICA

TRINIDAD & TOBAGO

PANAMA

VENEZUELA

GUYANA
SURINAME
FRENCH GUIANA (Fr)

CAPE VERDE

MAURITANIA

MALI
NIGER
CH

SENEGAL
GAMBIA
GUINEA-BISSAU
GUINEA

BURKINA
FASO

SIERRA LEONE
LIBERIA
IVORY
COAST
GHANA
BENIN
TOGO
NIGERIA

PACIFIC
OCEAN

COLOMBIA

ECUADOR

EQUATORIAL GUINEA
CAMEROON

SAO TOME & PRINCIPE
GABON
CONGO

PERU

BRAZIL

ANG

SCHOOLS AND SCHISMS

MOST POPULAR RELIGION BY GROUP AND SUB-GROUP

Buddhism

Mahayana   Theravada

Chinese   Tibetan   Japanese

BOLIVIA

NAMI

PARAGUAY

Christianity

Roman Catholicism   Orthodox

CHILE

Protestantism

Lutheranism   Anglicanism   Calvinism

URUGUAY

ARGENTINA

Methodism   Congregationalism   Baptist   Presbyterianism

Dutch Reform Church

OTHER RELIGIONS

Hinduism

Judaism

Chinese indigenous religion

other indigenous beliefs

official atheism

Islam

Sunni   Shia   Ibadiyyah

Hanafi   Hanbali   Maliki   Shafi

Ithna'ashaariyya   Zaydis

Sources: D.B. Barrett, *World Christian Encyclopedia*, 1982; F. Shaikh, ed. *Islam and Islamic Groups*, 1992; P. Harvey, *Introduction to Buddhism*, 1990

Yesterday's revolution can be today's orthodoxy. Some new movements have grown to become the most popular religion in a state.

RUSSIA

KAZAKHSTAN

MONGOLIA

see inset

TURKEY

UZBEK

TURKMEN

KIR

TAJ.

AFGHANISTAN

N·KOREA

JAPAN

S·KOREA

CHINA

AZER.

RUS.

SYRIA

LEBANON

ISRAEL

IRAQ

JOR.

KUWAIT

IRAN

BAHRAIN

QATAR

UAE

OMAN

PAKISTAN

NEPAL

BHUTAN

TAIWAN

PACIFIC OCEAN

SAUDI ARABIA

YPT

INDIA

'DESH

MYANMAR

MACAO

HONG KONG

LAOS

YEMEN

DAN

DJIBOUTI

THAILAND

VIETNAM

PHILIPPINES

CAM

SRI LANKA

KIRIBATI

ETHIOPIA

S.MALIA

KENYA

MALDIVES

BRUNEI

MALAYSIA

B.

TANZANIA

SEYCHELLES

SINGAPORE

INDIAN OCEAN

BOUGAINVILLE

COMOROS

PAPUA NEW GUINEA

SOLOMON ISLANDS

ALAWI

MAURITIUS

MADAGASCAR

REUNION

WESTERN SAMOA

AMERICAN SAMOA

MOZAMBIQUE

FIJI

TONGA

AUSTRALIA

NEW CALEDONIA

VANUATU

NEW ZEALAND

BLACK SEA

GEORGIA

AZERBAIJAN

TURKEY

ARMENIA

CYPRUS

LEBANON

SYRIA

IRAN

MEDITERRANEAN SEA

JORDAN

IRAQ

ISRAEL

KUWAIT

EGYPT

SAUDI ARABIA

RED SEA

BAHRAIN

Copyright © Myriad Editions Limited

ICELAND

NORWAY   SWEDEN   FIN

EST
LATV
DENMAR   LITH
IRELAND   BE
UNITED   NETH   POLAND   UK
KINGDOM   BEL   GERMANY
CZECH
REPUBLIC   SLOVAK
FRANCE   AUSTRIA   HUNGARY
S
ITALY   B-H   YUG
ALBANIA   M   BULGAR
GREECE
SPAIN
GIBRALTAR   MALTA

CANADA

UNITED STATES
OF AMERICA

BERMUDA

ATLANTIC
OCEAN

BAHAMAS
MEXICO
CUBA   DOMINICAN REPUBLIC
BELIZE   HAITI   PUERTO RICO (US)
JAMAICA
GUATEMALA   GUADELOUPE (Fr)
HONDURAS
EL SALVADOR   MARTINIQUE (Fr)
NICARAGUA   NETH. ANTILLES   GRENADA
COSTA RICA   BARBADOS
PANAMA   TRINIDAD & TOBAGO
GUYANA   CAPE VERDE
SURINAME
FRENCH GUIANA (Fr)

ECUADOR

PACIFIC
OCEAN

TUNISIA
MOROCCO
ALGERIA   LIBY
WESTERN SAHARA
MAURITANIA   MALI   NIGER   CH
SENEGAL
GAMBIA
GUINEA-BISSAU   BURKINA
GUINEA   FASO   NIGERIA
SIERRA LEONE   IVORY   GHANA   BENIN
COAST
LIBERIA   TOGO   CAMEROON
EQUATORIAL GUINEA
SAO TOME & PRINCIPE

ANG

CHI

URUGUAY

FALKLAND ISLANDS
(UK)

THE GLOBAL GIANTS

FOLLOWERS OF CHRISTIANITY AND
ISLAM percentages *1993*

proportion of population which is Christian	proportion of population which is Muslim
90%	90%
70%	70%
50%	50%

STATES WITH FEW CHRISTIANS OR
MUSLIMS

Christians and Muslims
both below 50 percent

Christians and Muslims
both below 30 percent

Christians and Muslims
both below 10 percent

Muslims less than 1 percent

Christians less than 1 percent

Sources: D.B. Barrett, ed. *World Christian
Encyclopedia*, 1982; D.B. Barrett, ed. *Our Globe
and How to Reach It*, 1990; I. Harris and others,
eds. *Contemporary Religions*, 1992; C. Horrie and
P.Chippindale, *What is Islam?*, 1990; F. Shaikh,
ed. *Islam and Islamic Groups*, 1992; press reports

Nearly half the world claims allegiance to the two
largest faiths: over a billion to Islam, nearly two billion
to Christianity.

RUSSIA

BELARUS

UKRAINE

KAZAKHSTAN

MONGOLIA

N KOREA

JAPAN

S KOREA

GEO

AZER

TURKEY

CYPRUS

LEBANON

SYRIA

ISRAEL

JOR

IRAQ

IRAN

TURKMEN

UZBEK

KIR

TAJ

AFGHANISTAN

CHINA

PACIFIC
OCEAN

KUWAIT

BAHRAIN

QATAR

UAE

OMAN

SAUDI ARABIA

YEMEN

DJIBOUTI

EGYPT

SUDAN

ETHIOPIA

SOMALIA

KENYA

PAKISTAN

NEPAL

BHUTAN

INDIA

B

DESH

MYANMAR

LAOS

THAILAND

CAM

VIETNAM

MACAO

HONG KONG

TAIWAN

PHILIPPINES

MARIANA
ISLANDS

KIRIBATI

MALDIVES

SRI LANKA

BRUNEI

MALAYSIA

SINGAPORE

INDONESIA

BOUGAINVILLE

SOLOMON
ISLANDS

SEYCHELLES

TANZANIA

COMOROS

MALAWI

MOZAMBIQUE

MADAGASCAR

MAURITIUS

REUNION

WESTERN SAMOA

FIJI

TONGA

NEW CALEDONIA

AUSTRALIA

NEW
ZEALAND

CANADA

UNITED STATES
OF AMERICA

575,000

MEXICO

BERMUDA

BAHAMAS

CUBA

BELIZE   HAITI   DOMINICAN REPUBLIC
GUATEMALA   HONDURAS JAMAICA   PUERTO RICO (US)
EL SALVADOR   GUADELOUPE (Fr)
         NICARAGUA   MARTINIQUE (Fr)
COSTA RICA   NETH. ANTILLES GRENADA   BARBADOS   300,000
         PANAMA   TRINIDAD & TOBAGO
VENEZUELA   GUYANA
         370,000   SURINAME
COLOMBIA   FRENCH GUIANA (Fr)

PACIFIC
OCEAN

ECUADOR

PERU

BRAZIL

BOLIVIA

PARAGUAY

CHILE

URUGUAY

ARGENTINA

FALKLAND ISLANDS
(UK)

ATLANTIC
OCEAN

GREENLAND
(Den)

ICELAND

NORWAY SWEDEN

IRELAND   UNITED
          KINGDOM   DENMARK
          500,000   NETH   PO
          BEL   GERMANY   CZ
          FRANCE   S   AUS
                   ITALY

PORTUGAL   SPAIN

GIBRALTAR (UK)
                   TUNISIA
MOROCCO

WESTERN SAHARA   ALGERIA   LIBY

CAPE VERDE   MAURITANIA   MALI   NIGER
          SENEGAL
GAMBIA
GUINEA-BISSAU   GUINEA   BURKINA
          SIERRA LEONE   IVORY   GHANA   FASO   NIGERIA
          LIBERIA   COAST   BENIN   TOGO
                   EQUATORIAL GUINEA   CAMEROON
                   SAO TOME & PRINCIPE   GABON
                            CONGO

                            ANG

                            NAM

HINDUS WORLDWIDE

NUMBER OF HINDUS PER STATE AS
A PROPORTION OF TOTAL
POPULATION *early 1990s*

number per 100,000
*actual number given for states with
over 300,000*

- 75,000
- 25,000
- 10,000
- 1000
- 500
- 250
- 100
- minimal number

Sources: D. B. Barrett , *World Christian
Encyclopedia*, 1982; R. Hinnells, ed.
A Handbook of Living Religions, 1984;
Ranchor Prime

HINDUS

LOCATION OF HINDUS AS
PROPORTION OF WORLD HINDU
POPULATION *1993*

world total: 695.5 million

South Asia
98.6%

rest of world
1.4%

There are nearly 750 million Hindus worldwide. Almost all live in South Asia. Many of the overseas communities have grown in areas linked to the trading routes of colonial powers.

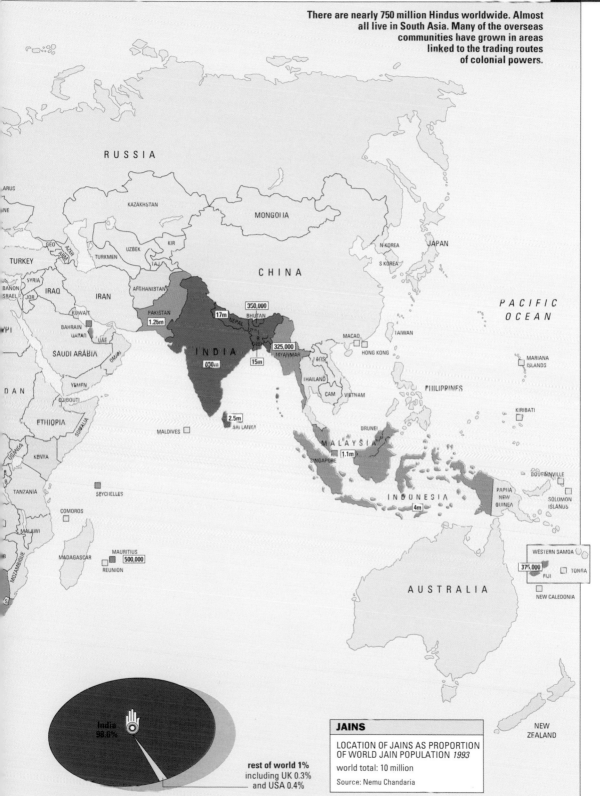

RUSSIA

KAZAKHSTAN

MONGOLIA

KIR

UZBEK

TURKMEN

TAJ

CHINA

N KOREA

JAPAN

S KOREA

TURKEY

GEO AZER

AFGHANISTAN

IRAN

PACIFIC OCEAN

SYRIA
LEBANON
ISRAEL JOR
IRAQ

KUWAIT
BAHRAIN
QATAR UAE

PAKISTAN
1.26m

350,000
17m
BHUTAN
NEPAL
15m

TAIWAN

MACAO
HONG KONG

MARIANA ISLANDS

SAUDI ARABIA

OMAN

YEMEN

DJIBOUTI

INDIA
630m

325,000
MYANMAR
15m

THAILAND

PHILIPPINES

CAM
VIETNAM

KIRIBATI

ETHIOPIA
SOMALIA

MALDIVES

2.5m
SRI LANKA

BRUNEI

MALAYSIA
1.1m

KENYA

SINGAPORE

TANZANIA

SEYCHELLES

INDONESIA
4m

PAPUA NEW GUINEA

BOUGAINVILLE

SOLOMON ISLANDS

COMOROS

MALAWI

MADAGASCAR

MAURITIUS
500,000
REUNION

WESTERN SAMOA

375,000
FIJI
TONGA

AUSTRALIA

NEW CALEDONIA

NEW ZEALAND

India
98.6%

rest of world 1%
including UK 0.3%
and USA 0.4%

JAINS

LOCATION OF JAINS AS PROPORTION OF WORLD JAIN POPULATION *1993*

world total: 10 million

Source: Nemu Chandaria

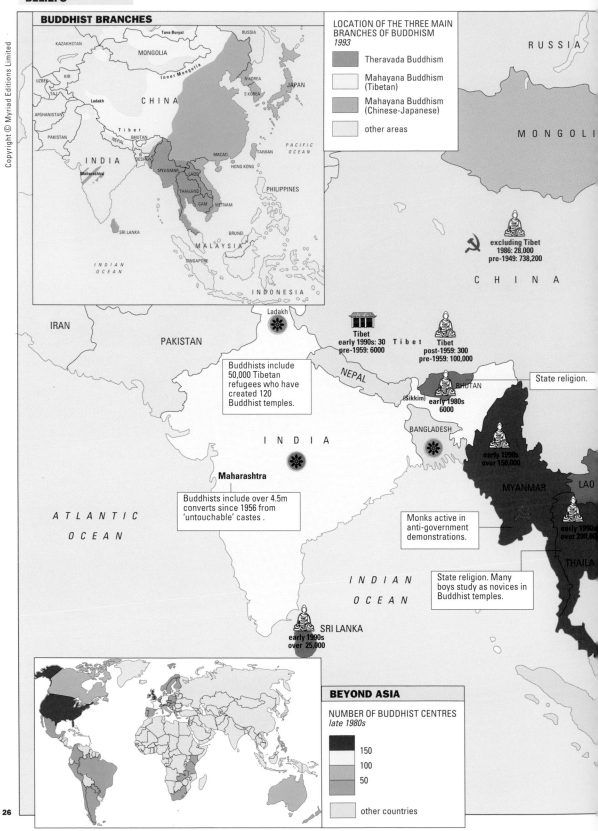

BUDDHIST BRANCHES

LOCATION OF THE THREE MAIN
BRANCHES OF BUDDHISM
1993

- Theravada Buddhism
- Mahayana Buddhism
  (Tibetan)
- Mahayana Buddhism
  (Chinese-Japanese)
- other areas

KAZAKHSTAN

MONGOLIA

Tuva Buryat

RUSSIA

UZBEK KIR

Inner Mongolia

TAJ. AFGHANISTAN

PAKISTAN

Ladakh

Tibet

CHINA

N.KOREA

S KOREA

JAPAN

NEPAL BHUTAN

DELHI

MACAO

TAIWAN

PACIFIC
OCEAN

INDIA

MYANMAR

LAOS

HONG KONG

Maharashtra

THAILAND

CAM

VIETNAM

PHILIPPINES

SRI LANKA

MALAYSIA

BRUNEI

SINGAPORE

INDIAN
OCEAN

INDONESIA

RUSSIA

MONGOLI

excluding Tibet
1986: 28,000
pre-1949: 738,200

CHINA

IRAN

PAKISTAN

Ladakh

Tibet
early 1990s: 30
pre-1959: 6000

Tibet
Tibet
post-1959: 300
pre-1959: 100,000

NEPAL

(Sikkim)

BHUTAN

early 1980s
6000

State religion.

BANGLADESH

Buddhists include
50,000 Tibetan
refugees who have
created 120
Buddhist temples.

INDIA

early 1990s
over 150,000

Maharashtra

MYANMAR

LAO

Buddhists include over 4.5m
converts since 1956 from
'untouchable' castes .

ATLANTIC

OCEAN

Monks active in
anti-government
demonstrations.

early 1990s
over 200,00

THAILA

INDIAN

OCEAN

State religion. Many
boys study as novices in
Buddhist temples.

SRI LANKA

early 1990s
over 25,000

BEYOND ASIA

NUMBER OF BUDDHIST CENTRES
late 1980s

- 150
- 100
- 50
- other countries

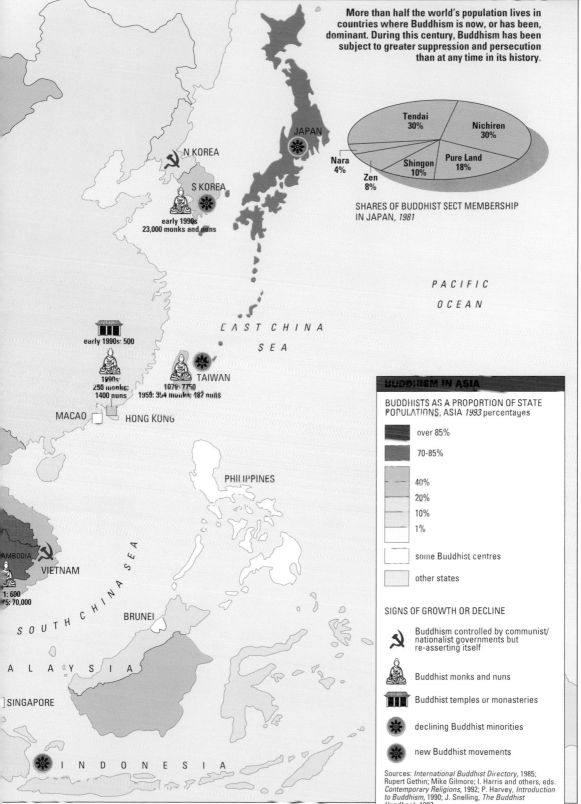

More than half the world's population lives in countries where Buddhism is now, or has been, dominant. During this century, Buddhism has been subject to greater suppression and persecution than at any time in its history.

JAPAN

N KOREA

S KOREA

early 1990s
23,000 monks and nuns

Tendai 30%

Nichiren 30%

Nara 4%

Zen 8%

Shingon 10%

Pure Land 18%

SHARES OF BUDDHIST SECT MEMBERSHIP IN JAPAN, *1981*

PACIFIC

OCEAN

EAST CHINA

SEA

early 1990s: 500

1990s
250 monks;
1400 nuns

1076: 7750
1959: 354 monks; 182 nuns

TAIWAN

MACAO

HONG KONG

PHILIPPINES

CAMBODIA

VIETNAM

1: 600
5: 70,000

SOUTH CHINA SEA

BRUNEI

MALAYSIA

SINGAPORE

INDONESIA

BUDDHISM IN ASIA

BUDDHISTS AS A PROPORTION OF STATE POPULATIONS, ASIA *1993* percentages

- over 85%
- 70-85%
- 40%
- 20%
- 10%
- 1%
- some Buddhist centres
- other states

SIGNS OF GROWTH OR DECLINE

Buddhism controlled by communist/ nationalist governments but re-asserting itself

Buddhist monks and nuns

Buddhist temples or monasteries

declining Buddhist minorities

new Buddhist movements

Sources: *International Buddhist Directory*, 1985; Rupert Gethin; Mike Gilmore; I. Harris and others, eds. *Contemporary Religions*, 1992; P. Harvey, *Introduction to Buddhism*, 1990; J. Snelling, *The Buddhist Handbook*, 1987

Copyright © Myriad Editions Limited

C A N A D A

U N I T E D   S T A T E S

O F   A M E R I C A

PUERTO RICO

MEXICO

COSTA RICA

PANAMA

COLOMBIA

ECUADOR

PERU

VENEZUELA

BRAZIL

ARGENTINA

URUGUAY

CHILE

THE DIASPORA

STATES' SHARES OF TOTAL
WORLD JEWISH POPULATION
1990

Size of state indicates its percen
share of world total: 12.8 million

= 1% (128,000)

= 0.1% (12,800

= 0.01% (1280

NUMBER OF JEWS IN EACH STA
PER 1000 POPULATION *1990*

	819
	22
	7
	5
	3

JEWS IN 1993

Europe
and
Russia
19.9%

North America
48.2%

Africa
1.2%

Central and South America
0.7%

Middle East
29.3%

JEWS IN 1800

0.003%
North
America

Europe
and
Russia
83.2%

9.1%

Africa 7.3%   Middle East

Oceania
0.7%

world total in 1800
3·28 million

world total in 1993
12.8 million

SHARES OF WORLD JEWISH POPULATION
BY REGION *1800 and 1993* percentages

=10%

=1%

=0.1%

Sources: D. Singer, ed. *The American
Jewish Yearbook*, 1992; Board of Depu
of British Jews

There are 12.8 million Jews worldwide who identify themselves as Jewish, though not all are religious Jews. Over 96 percent live in just 12 states.

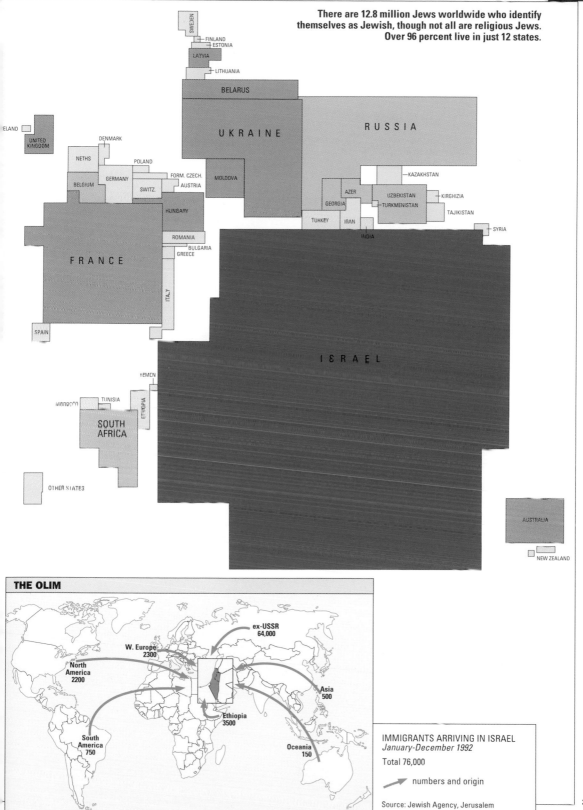

SWEDEN
FINLAND
ESTONIA
LATVIA
LITHUANIA
BELARUS
IRELAND
UNITED KINGDOM
DENMARK
UKRAINE
RUSSIA
NETHS
POLAND
BELGIUM GERMANY
SWITZ.
FORM. CZECH.
AUSTRIA
MOLDOVA
KAZAKHSTAN
AZER
UZBEKISTAN
KIRGHIZIA
GEORGIA
TURKMENISTAN
TAJIKISTAN
HUNGARY
TURKEY
IRAN
SYRIA
ROMANIA
BULGARIA
GREECE
INDIA
FRANCE
ITALY
ISRAEL
SPAIN
YEMEN
MOROCCO
TUNISIA
ETHIOPIA
SOUTH AFRICA
OTHER STATES
AUSTRALIA
NEW ZEALAND

THE OLIM

ex-USSR 64,000

W. Europe 2300

North America 2200

Asia 500

South America 750

Ethiopia 3500

Oceania 150

IMMIGRANTS ARRIVING IN ISRAEL
January-December 1992

Total 76,000

↗ numbers and origin

Source: Jewish Agency, Jerusalem

ICELAND

NORWAY

SWEDEN

1

DENMARK

LITH

ES

over 100

IRELAND

UNITED
KINGDOM

NETH

GERMANY

5

1

POLAND

CZECH
REPUBLIC

SLOVAK

BEL

FRANCE

1

SWITZ

AUSTRIA

HUNGARY

ROMA

S

C

ITALY

B-H

YUG

BUL

PORTUGAL

SPAIN

ALBANIA

M

GREECE

GIBRALTAR

MALTA

100

C A N A D A

50

U N I T E D   S T A T E S
O F   A M E R I C A

BERMUDA

MEXICO

BAHAMAS

ATLANTIC
OCEAN

TUNISIA

MOROCCO

ALGERIA

LIB

WESTERN SAHARA

CUBA

HAITI

DOMINICAN REPUBLIC

PUERTO RICO (US)

BELIZE

JAMAICA

GUATEMALA

HONDURAS

GUADELOUPE (Fr)

CAPE VERDE

MAURITANIA

MALI

NIGER

EL SALVADOR

NICARAGUA

MARTINIQUE (Fr)

NETH. ANTILLES

GRENADA

BARBADOS

SENEGAL

GAMBIA

GUINEA-BISSAU

GUINEA

BURKINA
FASO

C

COSTA RICA

TRINIDAD & TOBAGO

PANAMA

VENEZUELA

GUYANA

SURINAME

SIERRA LEONE

IVORY
COAST

GHANA

BENIN

NIGERIA

LIBERIA

PACIFIC
OCEAN

COLOMBIA

FRENCH GUIANA (Fr)

TOGO

EQUATORIAL GUINEA

CAMEROON

SAO TOME & PRINCIPE

GABON

1

ECUADOR

CONGO

PERU

B R A Z I L

AN

NA

BOLIVIA

PARAGUAY

CHILE

URUGUAY

ARGENTINA

FALKLAND ISLANDS
(UK)

SIKHS WORLDWIDE

STATES WITH SIGNIFICANT SIKH
POPULATIONS
1993

13 million

350,001-500,000

250,000- 350,000

25,000- 50,000

other states

number of Sikh gurdwaras
*a gurdwara is both a place
of worship and community
centre*

Sources: W. Owen Cole; Piara Singh
Sambhi; *Bahkshish Singh*; personal
communications

There are 16 million Sikhs worldwide.
Over 80 percent live in India, mainly in the Punjab.

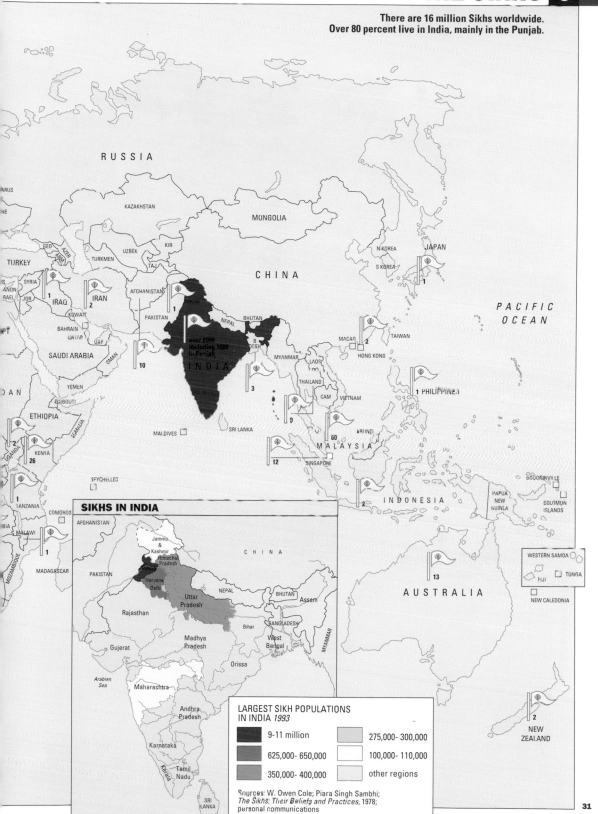

SIKHS IN INDIA

LARGEST SIKH POPULATIONS IN INDIA *1993*

■ 9-11 million	▨ 275,000- 300,000
▨ 625,000- 650,000	□ 100,000- 110,000
▨ 350,000- 400,000	□ other regions

Sources: W. Owen Cole; Piara Singh Sambhi;
The Sikhs: Their Beliefs and Practices, 1978;
personal communications

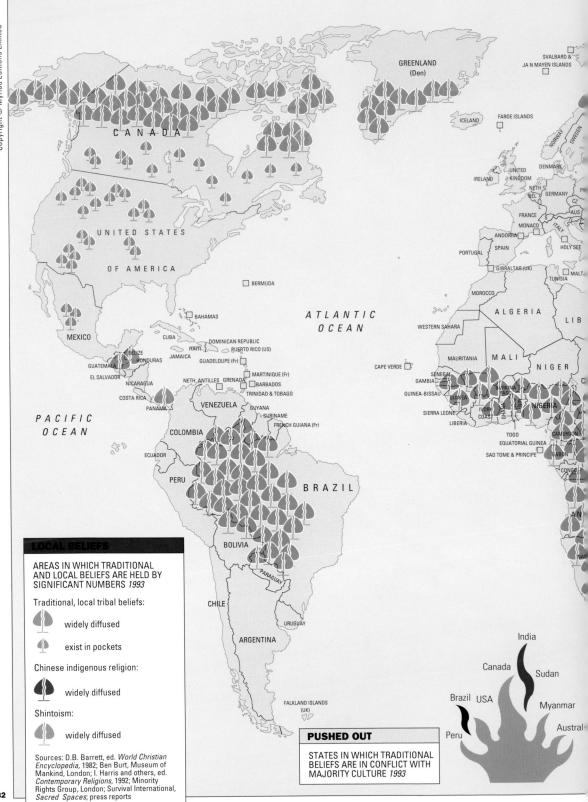

Copyright © Myriad Editions Limited

GREENLAND
(Den)

SVALBARD &
JA N MAYEN ISLANDS

ICELAND   FAROE ISLANDS

C A N A D A

NORWAY   SWEDEN

IRELAND   UNITED
KINGDOM   DENMARK

NETH   GERMANY   P
BEL

U N I T E D   S T A T E S

FRANCE   CZ
MONACO   AUS
S
ANDORRA   ITALY   HOLY SEE

O F   A M E R I C A

PORTUGAL   SPAIN

GIBRALTAR (UK)   MALT
TUNISIA

BERMUDA

MOROCCO

A T L A N T I C
O C E A N

ALGERIA   LIB

WESTERN SAHARA

MEXICO

BAHAMAS

CUBA
DOMINICAN REPUBLIC
HAITI   PUERTO RICO (US)
JAMAICA

MAURITANIA   M A L I   NIGER

CAPE VERDE

BELIZE
GUATEMALA   HONDURAS
EL SALVADOR
NICARAGUA

GUADELOUPE (Fr)

MARTINIQUE (Fr)

NETH. ANTILLES   GRENADA   BARBADOS
TRINIDAD & TOBAGO

SENEGAL
GAMBIA
GUINEA-BISSAU

SIERRA LEONE   IVORY
LIBERIA   COAST

BURKINA
FASO
GUINEA   GHANA   BENIN   NIGERIA

COSTA RICA
PANAMA

VENEZUELA

GUYANA
SURINAME

COLOMBIA

FRENCH GUIANA (Fr)

P A C I F I C
O C E A N

TOGO
EQUATORIAL GUINEA
SAO TOME & PRINCIPE   GABON

CAMEROON

CONGO

ECUADOR

AN

PERU

B R A Z I L

BOLIVIA

PARAGUAY

CHILE

URUGUAY

ARGENTINA

FALKLAND ISLANDS
(UK)

India
Canada   Sudan
Brazil   USA   Myanmar
Peru   Austral

PUSHED OUT

STATES IN WHICH TRADITIONAL
BELIEFS ARE IN CONFLICT WITH
MAJORITY CULTURE *1993*

Traditional and local beliefs vary widely. They are closely related to the land and have often survived where it is difficult or inaccessible. Many people belong to a major world religion while continuing to hold traditional local beliefs.

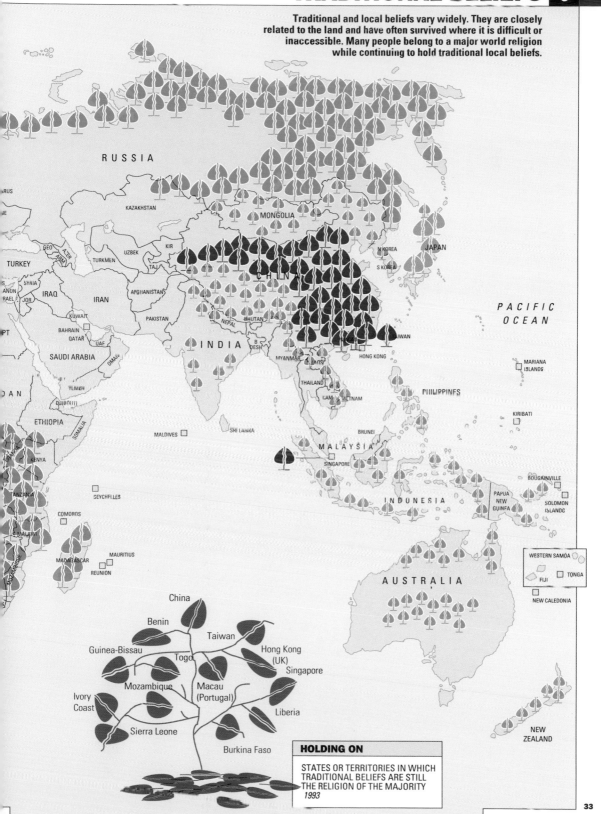

HOLDING ON

STATES OR TERRITORIES IN WHICH
TRADITIONAL BELIEFS ARE STILL
THE RELIGION OF THE MAJORITY
1993

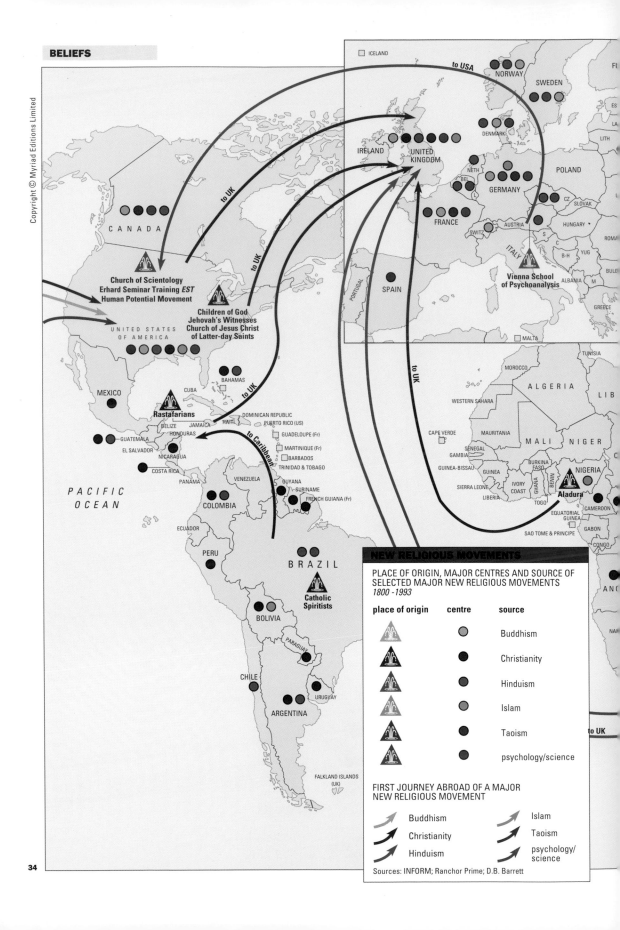

ICELAND

to USA
NORWAY
SWEDEN

DENMARK

IRELAND
UNITED
KINGDOM

NETH
BEL
GERMANY
POLAND

CZ
SLOVAK

FRANCE
AUSTRIA
HUNGARY
SWITZ

ITALY

Vienna School
of Psychoanalysis

ALBANIA

GREECE

MALTA

CANADA

Church of Scientology
Erhard Seminar Training *EST*
Human Potential Movement

Children of God
Jehovah's Witnesses
Church of Jesus Christ
of Latter-day Saints

UNITED STATES
OF AMERICA

to UK

to UK

PORTUGAL

SPAIN

to UK

TUNISIA

MOROCCO

ALGERIA

LIB

WESTERN SAHARA

MEXICO

CUBA
BAHAMAS

Rastafarians
BELIZE
JAMAICA
HAITI
HONDURAS
GUATEMALA
EL SALVADOR
NICARAGUA
COSTA RICA
PANAMA

DOMINICAN REPUBLIC
PUERTO RICO (US)
GUADELOUPE (Fr)
MARTINIQUE (Fr)
BARBADOS
TRINIDAD & TOBAGO

to Caribbean

to UK

VENEZUELA
GUYANA
SURINAME
FRENCH GUIANA (Fr)

CAPE VERDE

MAURITANIA

SENEGAL
GAMBIA
GUINEA-BISSAU
GUINEA
SIERRA LEONE
LIBERIA

MALI

BURKINA
FASO

IVORY
COAST

NIGER

GHANA
TOGO
BENIN

NIGERIA

Aladura

CAMEROON

PACIFIC
OCEAN

COLOMBIA

ECUADOR

PERU

B R A Z I L

Catholic
Spiritists

BOLIVIA

PARAGUAY

CHILE

URUGUAY

ARGENTINA

EQUATORIAL
GUINEA
SAO TOME & PRINCIPE

GABON
CONGO

ANG

to UK

FALKLAND ISLANDS
(UK)

NEW RELIGIOUS MOVEMENTS

PLACE OF ORIGIN, MAJOR CENTRES AND SOURCE OF
SELECTED MAJOR NEW RELIGIOUS MOVEMENTS
1800 - 1993

place of origin	centre	source
		Buddhism
		Christianity
		Hinduism
		Islam
		Taoism
		psychology/science

FIRST JOURNEY ABROAD OF A MAJOR
NEW RELIGIOUS MOVEMENT

Buddhism   Islam
Christianity   Taoism
Hinduism   psychology/
science

Sources: INFORM; Ranchor Prime; D.B. Barrett

The migration of people and ideas fosters 'new religious movements'. Most but not all have their origin in a major world religion. A small minority achieve a high profile as a result of unconventional and even criminal activities.

RUSSIA

KAZAKHSTAN

MONGOLIA

to USA
to USA
to USA

CHINA

N-KOREA
JAPAN
S KOREA

Unification Church

Soka Gakkai

PACIFIC OCEAN

TURKEY

IRAN

Baha'i to Haifa

Ahmadiya

AFGHANISTAN

PAKISTAN

NEPAL   BHUTAN

INDIA

B DESH

MYANMAR

MACAO   TAIWAN

HONG KONG

Taoist-influenced movements

MARIANA ISLANDS

SAUDI ARABIA

YEMEN

Brahma Kumaris International Society for Krishna Consciousness Sanyasins of Osho Transcendental Meditation

Human Potential Movement

LAOS

THAILAND

CAM   VIETNAM

PHILIPPINES

KIRIBATI

DAN

ETHIOPIA

Holy Spirit Movement

KENYA

SRI LANKA

MALDIVES

BRUNEI

MALAYSIA

SINGAPORE

INDIAN OCEAN

INDONESIA

many local movements with 60 m members

BOUGAINVILLE

PAPUA NEW GUINEA

SOLOMON ISLANDS

TANZANIA

SEYCHELLES

COMOROS

MALAWI

MADAGASCAR

MOZAMBIQUE

AUSTRALIA

WESTERN SAMOA

FIJI   TONGA

NEW CALEDONIA

to UK

Soka Gakkai
Nicheren Shoshu
20 m 1935

Transcendental Meditation
3 m 1958

Brahma Kumaris
World Spiritual University
350,000 1937

International Society for Krishna Consciousness
250,000 1965

Unification Church
1.1 m 1954

Children of God
25,000 1968

NEW ZEALAND

BIG SPRINGS

SELECTED 20TH CENTURY MOVEMENTS AND COUNTRY OF ORIGIN *1993*
Committed adherents and date founded

Japan   India   South Korea   USA

AMERICAN PIE

RELIGIOUS MAKE-UP OF THE USA
percentages *early 1990s*

Total number of separate Christian
denominations: 2550

Sources: D.B. Barrett, ed. *World
Christian Encyclopedia*, 1982

Protestant
52 %

Roman Catholic
30 %

Orthodox
Christian
2·2 %

marginal
Christian
3.6 %

Jewish
3·2 %

other
2·3 %

non-religious
6.7 %

C A N A D A

WASHINGTON

MONTANA

NORTH
DAKOTA

IDAHO

OREGON

SOUTH
DAKOTA

WYOMING

NEBRASKA

P A C I F I C
O C E A N

CALIFORNIA

NEVADA

UTAH

COLORADO

U N I T E D

O F   A

Sun Valley

BIB
8000

CALIFORNIA

Calvary Chapel
8000

Santa Monica

Calvary Chapel
8000
Downey

Riverside

Church of Christ
530%

Calvary Chapel
Santa Ana 12,000

ARIZONA

Los Angeles

Church of God in Christ
50%

Assemblies of God
10,500
Phoenix

NEW
MEXICO

Robert Schuller

1,2m

TV EVANGELISTS

THE TOP RELIGIOUS TELEVISION PROGRAMS,
USA *1991*
Number of viewing households and percentage
growth/decline since 1987

Sources: E. Draper, ed. *The Almanac of the Christian
World 1993-94,* 1992

TEXAS

The World Tomorrow

717,000

Kenneth Copeland

495,000

Oral Roberts

430,000

Charles Stanley

417,000

Jimmy Swaggart

348,000

D. James Kennedy

324,000

Jerry Falwell

303,000 (1990)

700 Club

198,000

M E X I C O

| − 6% | + 9.8% | + 31% | − 48% | + 45% | − 68% | − 12% | − 30% | − 37% |

Of all Christian traditions, Protestants have produced the greatest variety of denominations and churches, especially in the USA.

Christian and Missionary Alliance 40% — Crystal

Independent 13,000

Church of God 0.6 m

United Church of Christ 1.6 m — Cleveland

Independent Christian 76%

NEW YORK

MASS

CONN R.I.

VERMONT

MAINE

New York City

Episcopal 2.4 m

Independent Baptist 20,000 — Hammond

South Barrington

Chicago

PENNSYLVANIA

Philadelphia

Independent Christian 8000

Evangelical Lutheran 5.2 m

WISCONSIN

MINNESOTA

IOWA

INDIANA

OHIO

Washington D.C

Seventh Day Adventist 0.7 m

DEL

M.D

Indianapolis

Christian Church-Disciples of Christ 1.1 m

WEST VIRGINIA

VIRGINIA

ILLINOIS

MISSOURI

St Louis

Lutheran Missouri 2.6 m

KANSAS

KENTUCKY

NORTH CAROLINA

United Methodist 9 m — Nashville

Southern Baptist 14.9 m

Assemblies of God 2.1 m — Springfield

OKLAHOMA

ARKANSAS

Southern Baptist 43%

TENNESSEE

SOUTH CAROLINA

Presbyterian 29% — Atlanta

Presbyterian (USA) 2.9 m

Church of God in Christ 9000

College Park

Independent Christian 209%

MISSISSIPPI

ALABAMA

GEORGIA

ATLANTIC OCEAN

Southern Baptist 47%

LOUISIANA

FLORIDA

stin

Houston

Southern Baptist 8500

National Baptist 62.5%

United Methodist 65%

CUBA

MICHIGAN

TATES

RICA

PROTESTANT USA

THE WIDE RANGE OF PROTESTANTISM, USA *early 1990s*

There are 405,000 Christian places of worship in the USA, including 100,000 with no affiliation to any other group

🏛 largest denominations
headquarters and membership
1989 millions

🎵 largest churches
weekly attendance 1990

🎵 fastest growing congregations
1990 compared with 1989
percentages

Sources: John N. Vaughan; E. Draper, ed. *The Almanac of the Christian World 1993-94,* 1992

ICELAND

NORWAY

SWEDEN

FIN

IRELAND

UNITED
KINGDOM

Banneux
1933
8 occasions

DENMARK

Czestchowa
miraculous statue
worshipped since 1382

EST

LAT

LITH

Knock
1879
1 occasion

Walsingham
1061
1 occasion

NETH.

BEL

GERMANY

POLAND

B

UK

Pontmain
1871
1 occasion

Paris
1830
3 occasions

Beauraing
1932-33
33 occasions

CZECH
REPUBLIC

SLOVAK

AUSTRIA

HUNGARY

ROMANI

FRANCE

SWITZ

S

SPAIN

Lourdes
1858
18 occasions

La Salette
1846
1 occasion

ITALY

B-H

YUG

BULGA

PORTUGAL

Medjogorje
1881-93
many occasions

ALBANIA

M

GREECE

Fatima
1917
6 occasions

Garavandal
1961-65
several occasions

GIBRALTAR

MALTA

Mt A

C A N A D A

UNITED STATES
OF AMERICA

Necedah, Wisonsin
early 1950s
several occasions

Bayside, New York
early 1970s
many occasions

BERMUDA

A T L A N T I C
O C E A N

TUNISIA

MOROCCO

ALGERIA

LIBY

MEXICO

Mexico City
1531
4 occasions

BAHAMAS

CUBA

DOMINICAN REPUBLIC

HAITI

PUERTO RICO (US)

WESTERN SAHARA

BELIZE

GUATEMALA

HONDURAS

JAMAICA

GUADELOUPE (Fr)

MAURITANIA

M A L I

N I G E R

CH

EL SALVADOR

NICARAGUA

NETH. ANTILLES

MARTINIQUE (Fr)

BARBADOS

TRINIDAD & TOBAGO

CAPE VERDE

SENEGAL

GAMBIA

GUINEA-BISSAU

GUINEA

BURKINA
FASO

NIGERIA

COSTA RICA

PANAMA

VENEZUELA

GUYANA

SURINAME

FRENCH GUIANA (Fr)

SIERRA LEONE

IVORY
COAST

GHANA

BENIN

P A C I F I C
O C E A N

COLOMBIA

LIBERIA

TOGO

EQUATORIAL GUINEA

CAMEROON

ECUADOR

SAO TOME & PRINCIPE

GABON

CONGO

PERU

B R A Z I L

A N G

BOLIVIA

NAM

Aparecida do Tabuado
Basilica to Our Lady

PARAGUAY

CHILE

URUGUAY

ARGENTINA

FALKLAND ISLANDS
(UK)

THE FEMALE FORM

FEMALE DEITIES AND RELIGIOUS FIGURES IN
MAJOR RELIGIONS

states with a Roman Catholic majority:
tradition of devotion to the Virgin Mary

states with an Orthodox Christian majority:
tradition of devotion to the Mother of God

states with strong Buddhist tradition of devotion
to the Goddess of Mercy, Kuan Yin/Kwannon

states with strong Buddhist tradition of devotion
to the Tibetan Goddess Tara

states with Hindu majority:
tradition of devotion to the Goddess Kali

other states

Sources: A. Baring and J. Cashford, *The Myth of the Goddess,* 1991;
M.P. Carroll, *The Cult of the Virgin Mary,* 1992; J. Snelling,
The Buddhist Handbook, 1987

All major religions are patriarchal, though some contain within them strong devotional traditions associated with female deities or religious figures.

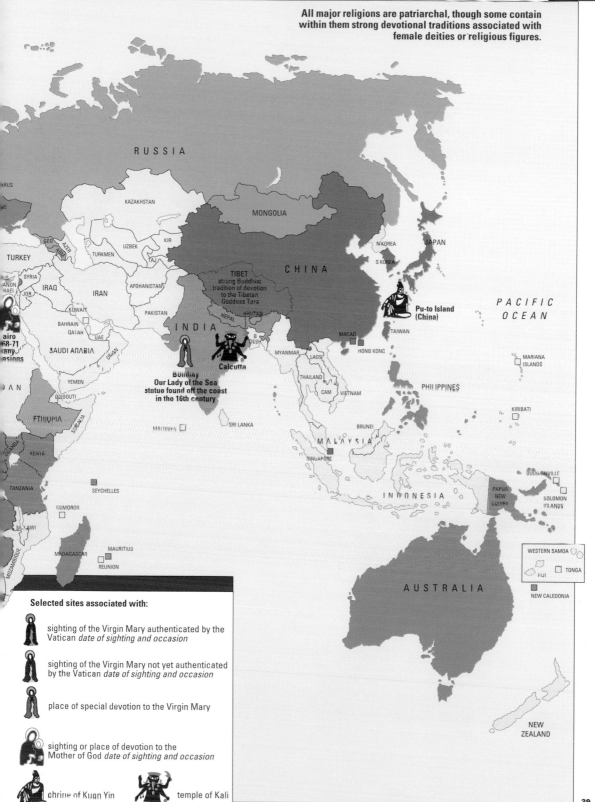

RUSSIA

KAZAKHSTAN

MONGOLIA

N.KOREA

JAPAN

S.KOREA

TURKEY

GEO

AZER

ARM

UZBEK

KIR

TURKMEN

TAJ

CHINA

PACIFIC
OCEAN

US

SYRIA

ANON

RAEL

IRAQ

JOR

IRAN

AFGHANISTAN

TIBET
strong Buddhist
tradition of devotion
to the Tibetan
Goddess Tara

Pu-to Island
(China)

KUWAIT

PAKISTAN

NEPAL

BHUTAN

BAHRAIN

QATAR

UAE

INDIA

B
DESH

MACAO

TAIWAN

airo
RR-71
any
asins

SAUDI ARABIA

OMAN

Calcutta

MYANMAR

HONG KONG

MARIANA
ISLANDS

AN

YEMEN

DJIBOUTI

Bombay
Our Lady of the Sea
statue found off the coast
in the 16th century

LAOS

THAILAND

CAM

VIETNAM

PHILIPPINES

KIRIBATI

ETHIOPIA

SOMALIA

MALDIVES

SRI LANKA

BRUNEI

UGANDA

KENYA

MALAYSIA

TANZANIA

SEYCHELLES

SINGAPORE

INDONESIA

BOUGAINVILLE

SOLOMON
ISLANDS

COMOROS

PAPUA
NEW
GUINEA

MALAWI

MADAGASCAR

MAURITIUS

REUNION

WESTERN SAMOA

MOZAMBIQUE

FIJI

TONGA

AUSTRALIA

NEW CALEDONIA

NEW
ZEALAND

Selected sites associated with:

sighting of the Virgin Mary authenticated by the Vatican *date of sighting and occasion*

sighting of the Virgin Mary not yet authenticated by the Vatican *date of sighting and occasion*

place of special devotion to the Virgin Mary

sighting or place of devotion to the Mother of God *date of sighting and occasion*

shrine of Kuan Yin

temple of Kali

Copyright © Myriad Editions Limited

ICELAND

NORWAY   SWEDEN   FI

DENMARK   LITH

IRELAND   EST

UNITED   NETH   POLAND
KINGDOM   BEL   GERMANY
        CZECH
        REPUBLIC   SLOVAK
FRANCE   SWITZ   AUSTRIA   HUNGARY   ROMA

        S   C

        ITALY   B-H   YUG   BULG

PORTUGAL   SPAIN   HOLY SEE   ALBANIA   M

        GREECE

GIBRALTAR   MALTA

C A N A D A

U N I T E D   S T A T E S
O F   A M E R I C A

BERMUDA

ATLANTIC
OCEAN

MEXICO

BAHAMAS

CUBA

BELIZE   HAITI   DOMINICAN REPUBLIC
        JAMAICA   PUERTO RICO (US)
GUATEMALA   HONDURAS   GUADELOUPE (Fr)
EL SALVADOR   MARTINIQUE (Fr)
NICARAGUA   NETH. ANTILLES   GRENADA
COSTA RICA   BARBADOS
    PANAMA   TRINIDAD & TOBAGO

CAPE VERDE

MOROCCO   TUNISIA

ALGERIA   LIB

WESTERN SAHARA

MAURITANIA   MALI   NIGER

SENEGAL
GAMBIA
GUINEA-BISSAU   BURKINA
    GUINEA   FASO
SIERRA LEONE   IVORY   GHANA   BENIN   NIGERIA
    COAST
LIBERIA   TOGO   CAMEROON
        EQUATORIAL GUINEA
        SAO TOME & PRINCIPE   GABON
            CONGO

PACIFIC
OCEAN

VENEZUELA   GUYANA
COLOMBIA   SURINAME
        FRENCH GUIANA (Fr)

ECUADOR

PERU

BRAZIL

BOLIVIA

PARAGUAY

CHILE

URUGUAY

ARGENTINA

A N

NA

FALKLAND ISLANDS
(UK)

HUMANISTS

HUMANIST ORGANIZATIONS *1993*

strong humanist organizatic
national organizations
with local groups
local organizations only
no organizations

headquarters of Internation
Humanist and Ethical Union

Sources: British Humanist Association;
International Humanist and Ethical Union

40

Over 20 percent of the world's population does not claim any allegiance to a religion. Most are agnostics. Others are atheists, who deny the existence of God.

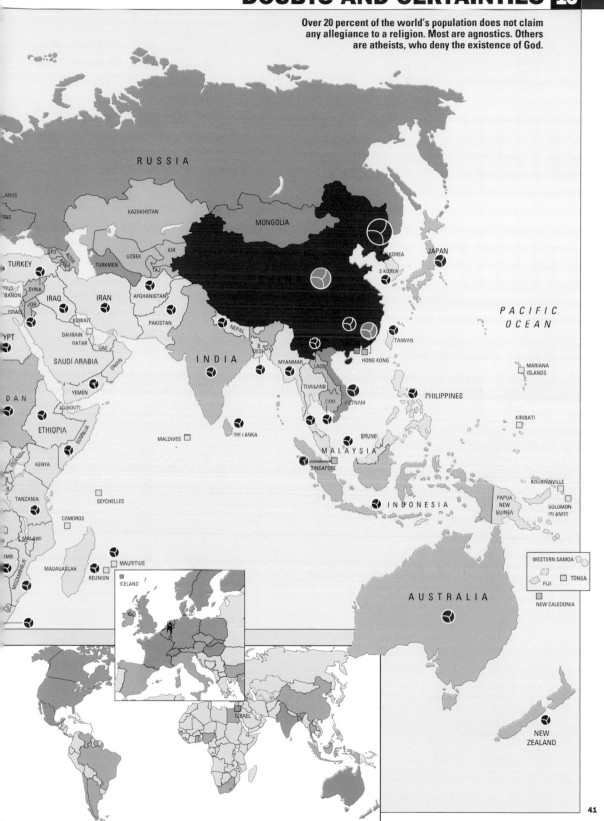

Part 2

REACHING OUT
CHALLENGES

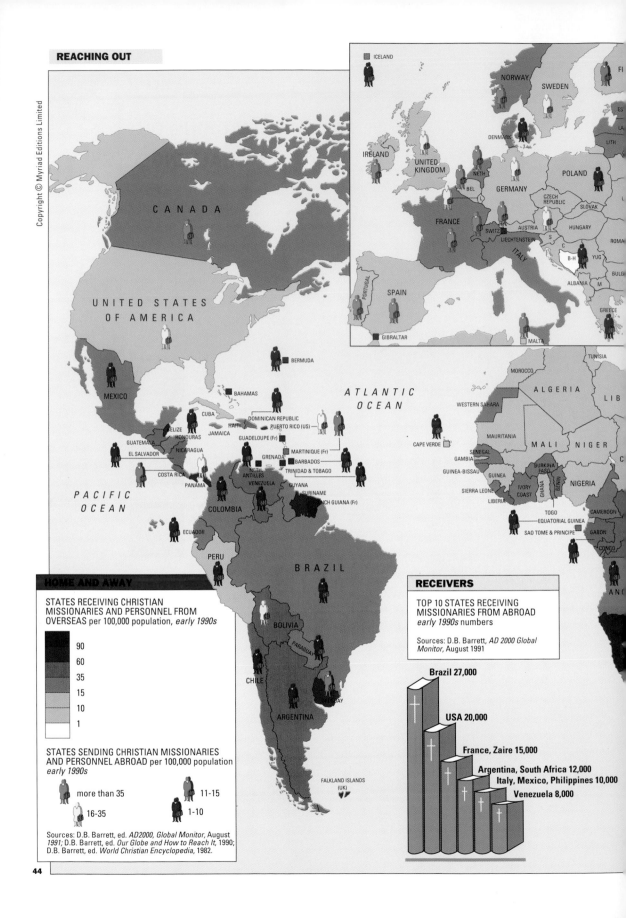

Copyright © Myriad Editions Limited

ICELAND

NORWAY   SWEDEN   FI

DENMARK

IRELAND   UNITED   NETH   POLAND

KINGDOM   BEL   GERMANY   CZECH

REPUBLIC   SLOVAK

FRANCE   SWITZ   AUSTRIA   HUNGARY   ROMA

LIECHTENSTEIN   S   C   ITALY   B-H   YUG   BULGI

PORTUGAL   SPAIN   ALBANIA   M

GREECE

GIBRALTAR   MALTA

ES

LA

LITH

CANADA

UNITED STATES
OF AMERICA

BERMUDA

BAHAMAS   ATLANTIC
OCEAN

MEXICO

CUBA

HAITI   DOMINICAN REPUBLIC
JAMAICA   PUERTO RICO (US)

BELIZE
HONDURAS   GUADELOUPE (Fr)

GUATEMALA   MARTINIQUE (Fr)
EL SALVADOR   NICARAGUA   GRENADA   BARBADOS

NETH.   TRINIDAD & TOBAGO
ANTILLES

COSTA RICA   VENEZUELA

PANAMA   GUYANA
SURINAME

PACIFIC
OCEAN   COLOMBIA   FRENCH GUIANA (Fr)

ECUADOR

PERU   BRAZIL

BOLIVIA

PARAGUAY

CHILE

URUGUAY

ARGENTINA

FALKLAND ISLANDS
(UK)

TUNISIA

MOROCCO   ALGERIA   LIB

WESTERN SAHARA

CAPE VERDE   MAURITANIA   MALI   NIGER

SENEGAL   C

GAMBIA   BURKINA
GUINEA-BISSAU   GUINEA   FASO   NIGERIA

SIERRA LEONE   IVORY   GHANA   BENIN
LIBERIA   COAST

TOGO   CAMEROON
EQUATORIAL GUINEA
SAO TOME & PRINCIPE   GABON
CONGO

ANG

STATES RECEIVING CHRISTIAN
MISSIONARIES AND PERSONNEL FROM
OVERSEAS per 100,000 population, *early 1990s*

90
60
35
15
10
1

STATES SENDING CHRISTIAN MISSIONARIES
AND PERSONNEL ABROAD per 100,000 population
early 1990s

more than 35   11-15

16-35   1-10

Sources: D.B. Barrett, ed. *AD2000, Global Monitor,* August
1991; D.B. Barrett, ed. *Our Globe and How to Reach It,* 1990;
D.B. Barrett, ed. *World Christian Encyclopedia,* 1982.

RECEIVERS

TOP 10 STATES RECEIVING
MISSIONARIES FROM ABROAD
early 1990s numbers

Sources: D.B. Barrett, *AD 2000 Global
Monitor,* August 1991

Brazil 27,000

USA 20,000

France, Zaire 15,000

Argentina, South Africa 12,000
Italy, Mexico, Philippines 10,000
Venezuela 8,000

There are more than 300,000 Christian missionaries worldwide. Some are evangelists only, but many work on social, health and education projects.

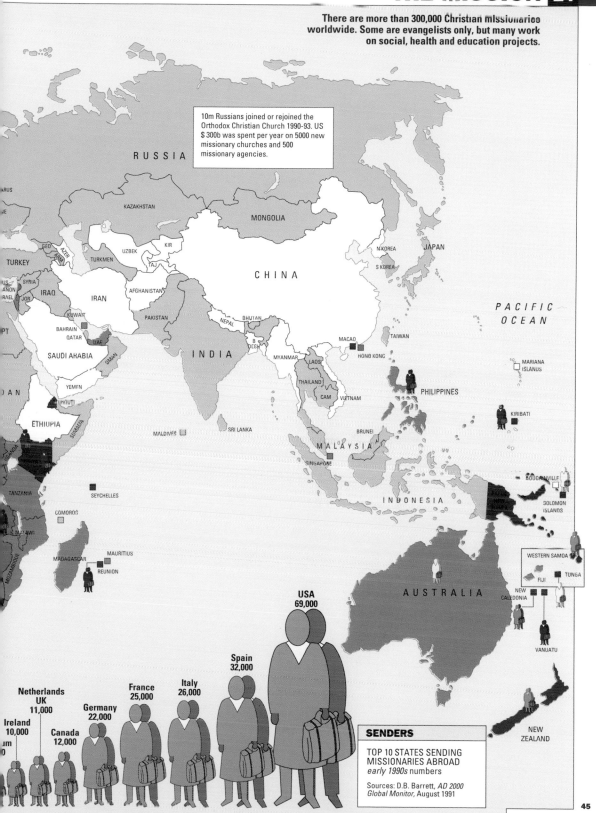

10m Russians joined or rejoined the Orthodox Christian Church 1990-93. US $300b was spent per year on 5000 new missionary churches and 500 missionary agencies.

RUSSIA

KAZAKHSTAN

MONGOLIA

N.KOREA JAPAN

S.KOREA

TURKEY

GEO AZER ARM

UZBEK KIR

TURKMEN

TAJ

IRAQ IRAN AFGHANISTAN

CHINA

PACIFIC OCEAN

KUWAIT

PAKISTAN

NEPAL BHUTAN

TAIWAN

BAHRAIN QATAR UAE

SAUDI ARABIA OMAN

INDIA

B DESH

MACAO

HONG KONG

MARIANA ISLANDS

YEMEN

MYANMAR

LAOS

DJIBOUTI

THAILAND

ETHIOPIA SOMALIA

CAM VIETNAM

PHILIPPINES

KIRIBATI

MALDIVES

SRI LANKA

BRUNEI

MALAYSIA

SEYCHELLES

SINGAPORE

COMOROS

INDONESIA

BOUGAINVILLE

SOLOMON ISLANDS

TANZANIA

PAPUA NEW GUINEA

MALAWI

MADAGASCAR MAURITIUS

REUNION

WESTERN SAMOA

MOZAMBIQUE

FIJI TONGA

NEW CALEDONIA

USA
69,000

AUSTRALIA

VANUATU

Spain
32,000

Netherlands
UK
11,000

France
25,000

Italy
26,000

NEW ZEALAND

Germany
22,000

Ireland
10,000

Canada
12,000

SENDERS

TOP 10 STATES SENDING MISSIONARIES ABROAD
early 1990s numbers

Sources: D.B. Barrett, *AD 2000 Global Monitor*, August 1991

Copyright © Myriad Editions Limited

ICELAND

NORWAY

SWEDEN

FI

DENMARK

IRELAND

UNITED KINGDOM

NETH

BEL

GERMANY

POLAND

CZECH REPUBLIC

SLOVAK

ES

LA

LITH

**To Europe
1979, 1980,
annual 1982-91**

FRANCE

SWITZ

AUSTRIA

HUNGARY

ROMA

S

C

YUG

ITALY

B-H

BULG

M

VATICAN

ALBANIA

GREECE

PORTUGAL

SPAIN

MALTA

CANADA

UNITED STATES
OF AMERICA

**To North America
1979, 1984, 1987**

BERMUDA

TUNISIA

MOROCCO

ALGERIA

LIB

WESTERN SAHARA

MEXICO

BAHAMAS

CUBA

DOMINICAN REPUBLIC

HAITI

PUERTO RICO (US)

**To Central America
1979, 1983,
1984, 1986,
1990, 1992**

**To Africa
1980, 1982, 1985
1988, 1989,
1990, 1992, 1993**

MAURITANIA

MALI

NIGER

BELIZE

GUATEMALA

HONDURAS

JAMAICA

GUADELOUPE (Fr)

CAPE VERDE

SENEGAL

EL SALVADOR

NICARAGUA

NETH. ANTILLES

MARTINIQUE (Fr)

GRENADA

BARBADOS

TRINIDAD & TOBAGO

GAMBIA

GUINEA-BISSAU

GUINEA

BURKINA
FASO

COSTA RICA

PANAMA

VENEZUELA

GUYANA

SURINAME

SIERRA LEONE

LIBERIA

IVORY
COAST

GHANA

BENIN

NIGERIA

*PACIFIC
OCEAN*

COLOMBIA

FRENCH GUIANA (Fr)

**To South America
1980, 1982,
annual 1985-88, 1991**

TOGO

CAMEROON

ECUADOR

SAO TOME &
PRINCIPE

GABON

CONGO

PERU

BRAZIL

EQUATORIAL
GUINEA

*ATLANTIC
OCEAN*

AN

BOLIVIA

PARAGUAY

NA

CHILE

URUGUAY

ARGENTINA

FALKLAND ISLANDS
(UK)

THE MASS FOR THE MASSES

CATHOLIC POPULATION PER PRIEST IN
CHRISTIAN MAJORITY COUNTRIES *1993*

- 100
- 500
- 1000
- 5000
- 10,000
- 15,000

no data

other states

state visits by the Pope,
1979 to early 1993

Sources: F.A.Foy, ed. *Catholic Almanac*, 1993;
*The Statistical Yearbook of the Church 1993;
Annuario Pontificio 1992*

The Pope heads a global network which stretches out to 900 million Roman Catholics, one-sixth of the world's population.

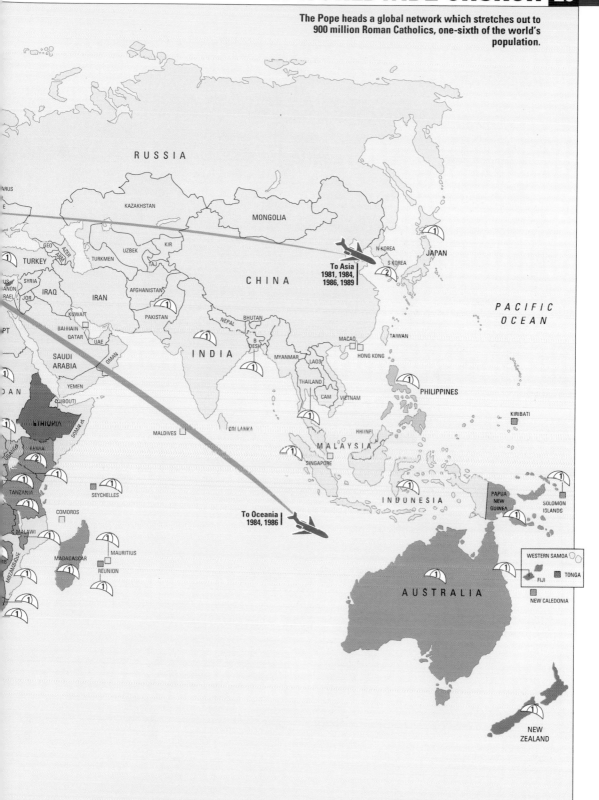

To Asia
1981, 1984,
1986, 1989

To Oceania
1984, 1986

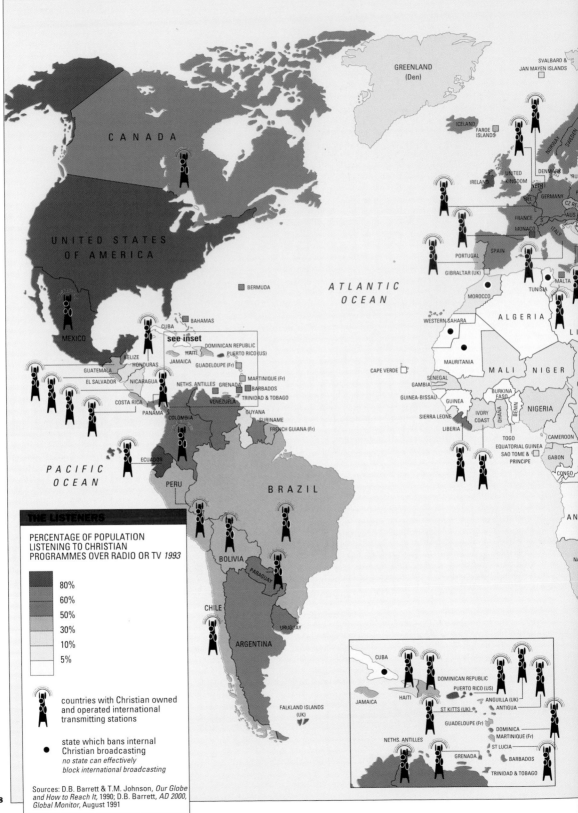

GREENLAND
(Den)

SVALBARD &
JAN MAYEN ISLANDS

CANADA

ICELAND

FAROE
ISLANDS

NORWAY   SWEDEN

IRELAND   UNITED
KINGDOM

DENMARK   RUS

NETH   GERMANY   CZ REF

BEL   AUS

FRANCE   S   ITALY

MONACO

UNITED STATES
OF AMERICA

BERMUDA

ATLANTIC
OCEAN

PORTUGAL   SPAIN

GIBRALTAR (UK)

MALTA

TUNISIA

MOROCCO

MEXICO

CUBA   BAHAMAS

see inset

DOMINICAN REPUBLIC
PUERTO RICO (US)

HAITI

JAMAICA

GUADELOUPE (Fr)

BELIZE   HONDURAS

GUATEMALA

EL SALVADOR   NICARAGUA

COSTA RICA

PANAMA

MARTINIQUE (Fr)

NETHS. ANTILLES   GRENADA   BARBADOS

VENEZUELA   TRINIDAD & TOBAGO

COLOMBIA

GUYANA

SURINAME

FRENCH GUIANA (Fr)

WESTERN SAHARA

CAPE VERDE

MAURITANIA

ALGERIA

LI

MALI   NIGER

SENEGAL

GAMBIA

GUINEA-BISSAU

GUINEA

BURKINA
FASO

BENIN

NIGERIA

SIERRA LEONE

IVORY
COAST

GHANA

TOGO

ECUADOR

PACIFIC
OCEAN

PERU

BRAZIL

LIBERIA

EQUATORIAL GUINEA

SAO TOME &
PRINCIPE

CAMEROON

GABON

CONGO

AN

BOLIVIA

PARAGUAY

CHILE

URUGUAY

ARGENTINA

FALKLAND ISLANDS
(UK)

NA

THE LISTENERS

PERCENTAGE OF POPULATION
LISTENING TO CHRISTIAN
PROGRAMMES OVER RADIO OR TV *1993*

- 80%
- 60%
- 50%
- 30%
- 10%
- 5%

countries with Christian owned
and operated international
transmitting stations

● state which bans internal
Christian broadcasting
*no state can effectively
block international broadcasting*

Sources: D.B. Barrett & T.M. Johnson, *Our Globe
and How to Reach It,* 1990; D.B. Barrett, *AD 2000,
Global Monitor,* August 1991

CUBA

DOMINICAN REPUBLIC
PUERTO RICO (US)

JAMAICA   HAITI

ANGUILLA (UK)

ANTIGUA

ST KITTS (UK)

GUADELOUPE (Fr)

DOMINICA

MARTINIQUE (Fr)

ST LUCIA

NETHS. ANTILLES

GRENADA

BARBADOS

TRINIDAD & TOBAGO

The only regular contact many Christians have with their own faith is via radio and television. While Christian broadcasting is aimed at and reaches every country in the world, 99.9 percent is produced for those where most people are already Christian.

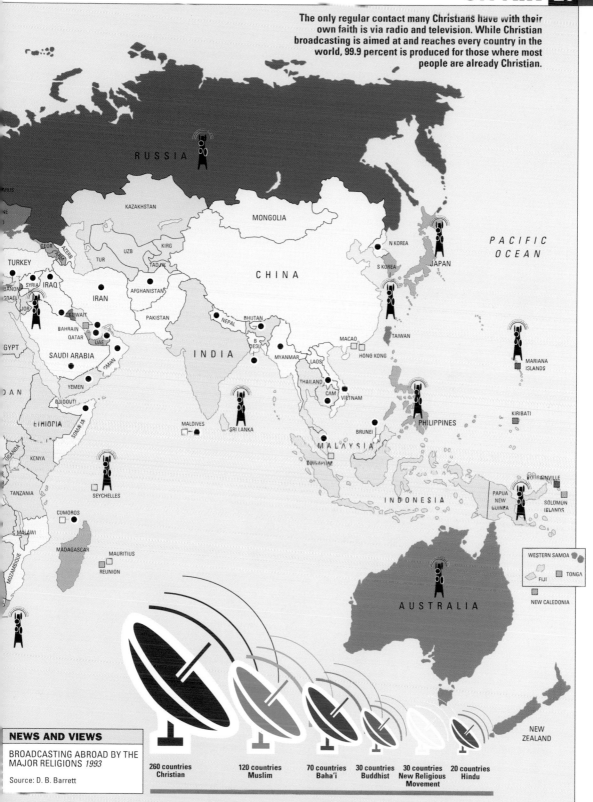

RUSSIA

KAZAKHSTAN

MONGOLIA

PACIFIC OCEAN

TURKEY

GEOR

AZERB

UZB

KIRG

TUR

TADJIK

N KOREA

S KOREA

JAPAN

LEBANON

SYRIA

IRAQ

IRAN

AFGHANISTAN

C H I N A

ISRAEL

JOR

KUWAIT

PAKISTAN

NEPAL

BHUTAN

MACAO

TAIWAN

BAHRAIN

QATAR

UAE

B DESH

HONG KONG

EGYPT

SAUDI ARABIA

OMAN

I N D I A

MYANMAR

LAOS

MARIANA ISLANDS

SUDAN

YEMEN

THAILAND

CAM

VIETNAM

DJIBOUTI

MALDIVES

SRI LANKA

KIRIBATI

ETHIOPIA

SOMALIA

BRUNEI

PHILIPPINES

UGANDA

KENYA

M A L A Y S I A

TANZANIA

SEYCHELLES

SINGAPORE

BOUGAINVILLE

COMOROS

I N D O N E S I A

PAPUA NEW GUINEA

SOLOMON ISLANDS

S MALAWI

MOZAMBIQUE

MADAGASCAR

MAURITIUS

REUNION

WESTERN SAMOA

FIJI

TONGA

A U S T R A L I A

NEW CALEDONIA

NEW ZEALAND

NEWS AND VIEWS

BROADCASTING ABROAD BY THE MAJOR RELIGIONS *1993*

Source: D. B. Barrett

260 countries Christian

120 countries Muslim

70 countries Baha'i

30 countries Buddhist

30 countries New Religious Movement

20 countries Hindu

Copyright © Myriad Editions Limited

ICELAND

NORWAY

SWEDEN

FIN

EST

UNITED
KINGDOM

DENMARK

LITH

$ 65 m

IRELAND

$ 71 m

$ 21 m

GERMANY

POLAND

U

NETH

$ 104 m

$ 39m

BEL

CZECH
REPUBLIC

SLOVAK

C A N A D A

FRANCE

$ 73 m

AUSTRIA

HUNGARY

ROMA

SWITZ

S

B-H

YUG

ITALY

C

YUG

UNITED STATES
OF AMERICA

BULG

$ 256 m

SPAIN

ALBANIA

M

PORTUGAL

GREECE

BERMUDA

GIBRALTAR

MALTA

TUNISIA

MOROCCO

ATLANTIC
OCEAN

BAHAMAS

ALGERIA

LIB

CUBA

WESTERN SAHARA

DOMINICAN REPUBLIC

HAITI

PUERTO RICO (US)

MEXICO

BELIZE

JAMAICA

GUADELOUPE (Fr)

CAPE VERDE

MAURITANIA

MALI

NIGER

GUATEMALA

HONDURAS

SENEGAL

EL SALVADOR

MARTINIQUE (Fr)

GAMBIA

NICARAGUA

NETH. ANTILLES

GRENADA

BARBADOS

GUINEA-BISSAU

BURKINA
FASO

COSTA RICA

TRINIDAD & TOBAGO

GUINEA

NIGERIA

PANAMA

VENEZUELA

GUYANA

SIERRA LEONE

IVORY
COAST

GHANA

BENIN

SURINAME

LIBERIA

PACIFIC
OCEAN

COLOMBIA

FRENCH GUIANA (Fr)

TOGO

CAMEROON

EQUATORIAL GUINEA

ECUADOR

SAO TOME & PRINCIPE

GABON

CONGO

PERU

B R A Z I L

AN

BOLIVIA

NA

PARAGUAY

CHILE

URUGUAY

ARGENTINA

FALKLAND
ISLANDS
(UK)

Sources: Agency yearbooks, annual reports, financial statements, 1991

GIVE AND TAKE

SELECTED CHRISTIAN AID AGENCIES AND
ANNUAL EXPENDITURES *1991*
located by agency headquarters

Evangelische Zentralstelle für
Entwicklingshilfe E.V.
(EZE)

Christian Aid

Catholic Fund for Overseas Development
(CAFOD)

World Vision International

donor to World Vision International

Danchurchaid

Brot für die Welt

Stichting Oecumenische Hulp

Christian World Service

STATES RECEIVING CHRISTIAN AID FROM
ABOVE AGENCIES *1991*

from 7 or 8 agencies		2	
5 or 6		1	
3 or 4		other states	

There are thousands of Christian aid agencies worldwide. These are among the largest. Aid is not usually given on the basis of religious affiliation.

RUSSIA

KAZAKHSTAN

MONGOLIA

N KOREA

JAPAN

S KOREA

UZBEK   KIR

TURKMEN

TAJ

CHINA

TURKEY

GEO
AZER
ARM

SYRIA   IRAQ   IRAN   AFGHANISTAN

LEBANON
ISRAEL   JOR

KUWAIT

BAHRAIN
QATAR   UAE

SAUDI ARABIA   OMAN

YEMEN

DJIBOUTI

ETHIOPIA   SOMALIA

KENYA

TANZANIA   SEYCHELLES

COMOROS

MALAWI

MADAGASCAR   MAURITIUS

REUNION

MOZAMBIQUE

PAKISTAN   NEPAL   BHUTAN

INDIA

MYANMAR   LAOS

THAILAND

CAM   VIETNAM

MACAO

HONG KONG   TAIWAN

MALDIVES   SRI LANKA

INDIAN OCEAN

BRUNEI

MALAYSIA

SINGAPORE

INDONESIA

PHILIPPINES

PACIFIC OCEAN

MARIANA ISLANDS

KIRIBATI

BOUGAINVILLE

PAPUA NEW GUINEA   SOLOMON ISLANDS

AUSTRALIA

WESTERN SAMOA

FIJI   TONGA

NEW CALEDONIA

$ 0.9 m

NEW ZEALAND

HELPLINE

BREAKDOWN OF AID GIVEN BY BROT FÜR DIE WELT, *1991*
percentages

Source: Brot für die Welt, 1991

personal aid/
self-reliance
38%

health/education/
social
34%

human rights
3%

emergency

10%

other
12%

technical
3%

GREENLAND
(Den)

SVALBARD &
JAN MAYEN ISLANDS

ICELAND

FAROE ISLANDS

NORWAY SWEDEN

CANADA

IRELAND

UNITED
KINGDOM

NETH
BEL

DENMARK

GERMANY

PO

CZ

UNITED STATES
OF AMERICA

FRANCE

ITALY

PORTUGAL SPAIN

GIBRALTAR (UK)

BERMUDA

MALTA

TUNISIA

MOROCCO

ATLANTIC
OCEAN

MEXICO

BAHAMAS

CUBA

DOMINICAN REPUBLIC
PUERTO RICO (US)

HAITI

BELIZE

HONDURAS

JAMAICA

GUADELOUPE (Fr)

GUATEMALA

EL SALVADOR

MARTINIQUE (Fr)

NICARAGUA

NETH. ANTILLES GRENADA

BARBADOS

COSTA RICA

TRINIDAD & TOBAGO

PANAMA

VENEZUELA

GUYANA

SURINAME

COLOMBIA

FRENCH GUIANA (Fr)

ECUADOR

PERU

BRAZIL

PACIFIC
OCEAN

CAPE VERDE

WESTERN SAHARA

ALGERIA

LIB

MAURITANIA

MALI

NIGER

SENEGAL

GAMBIA

GUINEA-BISSAU

GUINEA

BURKINA
FASO

C

SIERRA LEONE

IVORY
COAST

GHANA

BENIN

NIGERIA

LIBERIA

TOGO

CAMEROON

EQUATORIAL GUINEA

SAO TOME & PRINCIPE

GABON

CONGO

ANG

BOLIVIA

PARAGUAY

NAM

CHILE

URUGUAY

ARGENTINA

FALKLAND ISLANDS
(UK)

ZAKAT

FOUNDING COUNTRY AND DONORS TO FIVE
INTERNATIONAL MUSLIM AID AGENCIES
1991-92

Muslim Aid
founded 1985

donor to Muslim Aid

Human Appeal International
founded 1984

donor to Human Appeal International

Islamic Relief
founded 1984

donor to Islamic Relief

Islamic Relief Agency
founded 1987

donor to Islamic Relief Agency

Edhi International Foundation
founded 1950

donor to Edhi International Foundation

STATES RECEIVING INTERNATIONAL MUSLIM
DEVELOPMENT AND EMERGENCY AID FROM
ABOVE AGENCIES *1991-92*

from 5 agencies

4

3

2

1

other states

Sources: *Q News Magazine*; Agency annual reports and financial statements

The giving of zakat – part of personal wealth which must be given each year for charity – is one of the Five Pillars of Islam. International Muslim aid agencies have recently emerged to fund development aid to areas of need.

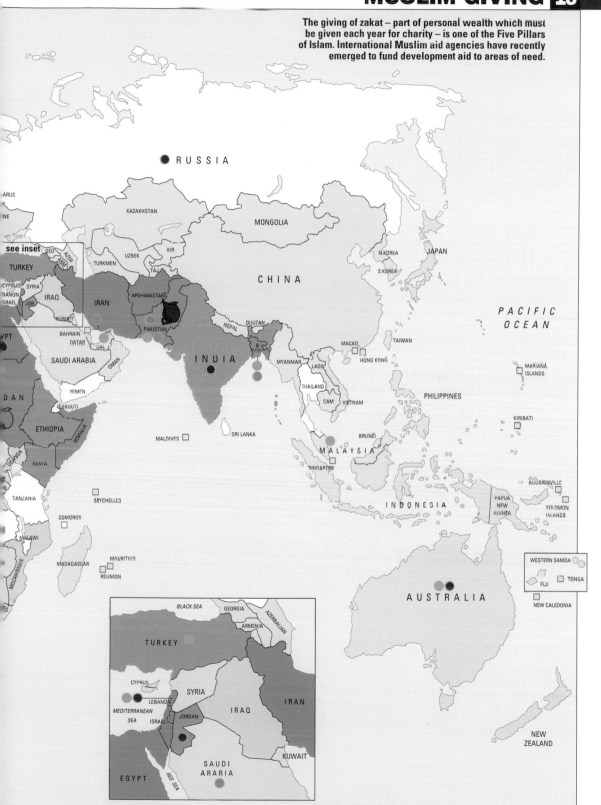

STATES IN WHICH SOME FORM OF
ISLAMIC BANKING IS PRACTISED
1993

states attempting to restructure
national banking in accordance
with Islamic law – Shari'ah

other states where Islam is the
religion of the majority

non-Muslim states with some
form of Islamic banking

other non-Muslim states

THE BANKS

banks whose systems are
based on Islamic principles
bank named

number of other national banks
which offer some form of Islamic
non-usury banking as part
of service

Sources: Annual reports of banks; International
Association of Islamic Banks; Fazlun Khalid

The Qur'an forbids the charging and taking of interest. Some countries are working to create an Islamic non-usury form of banking. Strict application of Islamic law would mean that all trade would be by barter or exchange of precious metals. Ultimately, paper money and the whole notion of banking are alien to Islam.

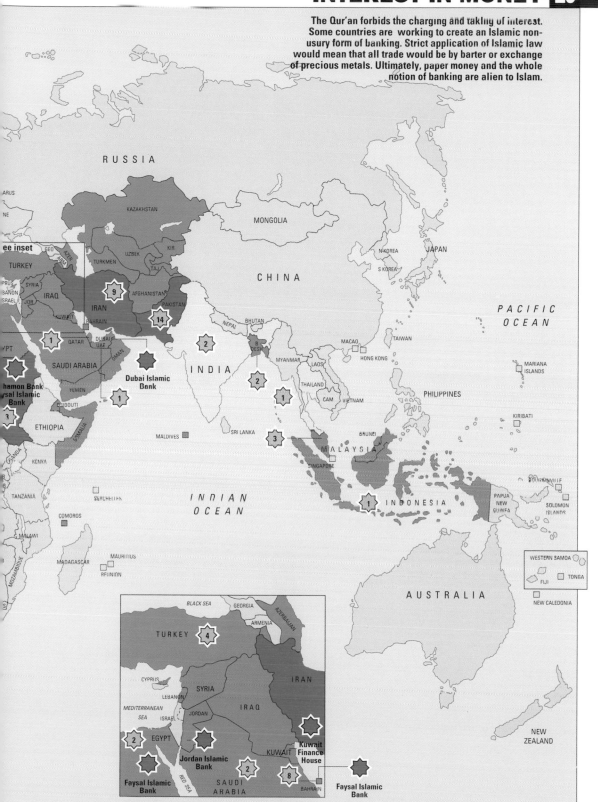

ICELAND

NORWAY

Lutheranism
Christianity and
all other religions

Lutheranism
Christianity

SWEDEN

Lutheranism
Christianity

Lutheranism
Orthodox Church
of Finland
Christianity

Church of Sweden
Christianity

Church of England
Church of Scotland
Christianity

DENMARK

Roman Catholicism
Judaism
Islam
Protestantism
Anglicanism

LITH.

IRELAND

UNITED
KINGDOM

GERMANY

POLAND

NETH.

BEL

FRANCE

CZECH
REPUBLIC

SLOVAK

AUSTRIA

HUNGARY

SWITZ

ITALY

PORTUGAL

SPAIN

HOLY SEE

CROATIA

B-H

YUG

ROMA

ALBANIA

M

BULGA

Roman Catholicism

GREECE

B.
Or
Che

GIBRALTAR

Roman Catholicism

MALTA

Church of Greece
Christianity

TUNISIA

CANADA

UNITED STATES
OF AMERICA

BERMUDA

ATLANTIC
OCEAN

MOROCCO

Islam

Islam

Islam

WESTERN SAHARA

Islam

ALGERIA

Islam

BAHAMAS

MEXICO

CUBA

HAITI

DOMINICAN REPUBLIC

PUERTO RICO (US)

BELIZE

HONDURAS

JAMAICA

GUATEMALA

EL SALVADOR

Roman
Catholicism

NICARAGUA

Roman
Catholicism

COSTA RICA

PANAMA

GUADELOUPE (Fr)

MARTINIQUE (Fr)

NETH. ANTILLES GRENADA

BARBADOS

TRINIDAD & TOBAGO

VENEZUELA

GUYANA

SURINAME

FRENCH GUIANA (Fr)

COLOMBIA

ECUADOR

PERU

BRAZIL

MAURITANIA

Islam

MALI

NIGER

C

CAPE VERDE

SENEGAL

GAMBIA

GUINEA-BISSAU

GUINEA

SIERRA LEONE

IVORY
COAST

BURKINA
FASO

LIBERIA

GHANA

BENIN

NIGERIA

TOGO

EQUATORIAL GUINEA

SAO TOME & PRINCIPE

CAMEROON

GABON

CONGO

PACIFIC
OCEAN

Roman
Catholicism

BOLIVIA

PARAGUAY

Roman
Catholicism

AN

NAM

CHILE

Roman
Catholicism

URUGUAY

ARGENTINA

FALKLAND ISLANDS
(UK)

FREEDOM AND RESTRICTION

STATE ATTITUDES TO THE RELIGION OF THE
MAJORITY AND OTHER RELIGIONS *1993*

discriminates against all religions
and interferes with religious freedom

favours religion of majority and interferes
with or limits freedom of other religions

favours religion of majority but
tolerates other religions

tolerates all religions

unclear or unknown

state declared atheist in law

state religion established in law

state recognizes more than one religion
or religious group

state attitude to religion liable to change

monarch must be of given faith

head of state or government must be
of given faith

Sources: D. Barrett, ed. *World Christian Encyclopedia*, 1982;
F. Shaikh, ed. *Islam and Islamic Groups*, 1992;
B. Szaijkowski ed. *New Political Parties of Eastern Europe
and the Soviet Union*, 1992; press reports

Nearly a quarter of the world's states have formal links with a religion. Three states have links with more than one. A few states, including those officially atheist, actively discriminate against all religions.

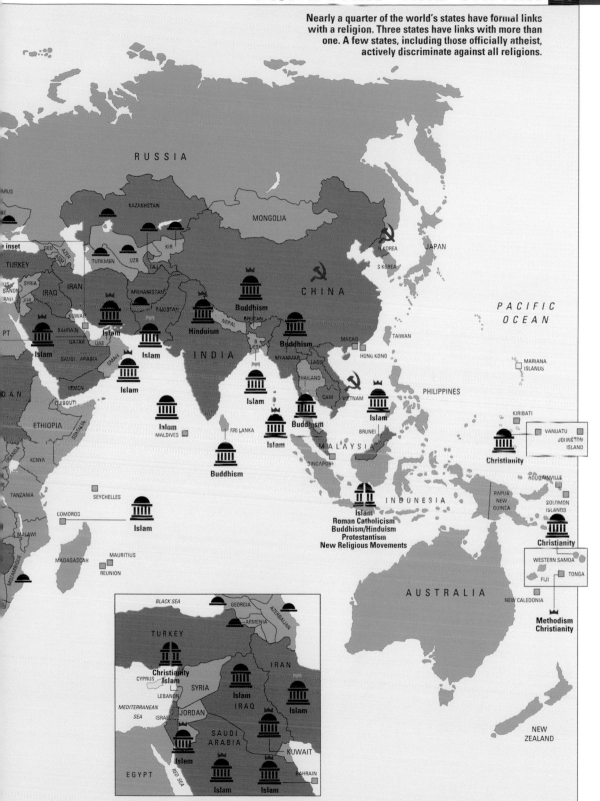

RUSSIA

KAZAKHSTAN

MONGOLIA

N KOREA

JAPAN

S KOREA

CHINA

PACIFIC OCEAN

TURKMEN

UZB

TAJ

AFGHANISTAN

PAKISTAN

NEPAL

BHUTAN

Buddhism

Hinduism

INDIA

B DESH

MYANMAR

Buddhism

MACAO

TAIWAN

HONG KONG

MARIANA ISLANDS

SYRIA

IRAN

IRAQ

KUWAIT

BAHRAIN

QATAR

UAE

OMAN

Islam

SAUDI ARABIA

YEMEN

Islam

Islam

THAILAND

LAOS

CAM

VIETNAM

Islam

PHILIPPINES

KIRIBATI

JIBOUTI

Islam

SRI LANKA

Islam

Buddhism

BRUNEI

MALAYSIA

VANUATU

JOHNSTON ISLAND

ETHIOPIA

SOMALIA

MALDIVES

SINGAPORE

Christianity

KENYA

Buddhism

BOUGAINVILLE

TANZANIA

SEYCHELLES

INDONESIA

PAPUA NEW GUINEA

SOLOMON ISLANDS

COMOROS

Islam

Islam
Roman Catholicism
Buddhism/Hinduism
Protestantism
New Religious Movements

Christianity

MALAWI

MADAGASCAR

MAURITIUS

REUNION

WESTERN SAMOA

FIJI

TONGA

MOZAMBIQUE

AUSTRALIA

NEW CALEDONIA

Methodism
Christianity

NEW ZEALAND

BLACK SEA

GEORGIA

AZERBAIJAN

ARMENIA

TURKEY

IRAN

Christianity
Islam

CYPRUS

LEBANON

SYRIA

Islam

IRAQ

Islam

MEDITERRANEAN SEA

ISRAEL

JORDAN

SAUDI ARABIA

KUWAIT

Islam

EGYPT

RED SEA

Islam

Islam

BAHRAIN

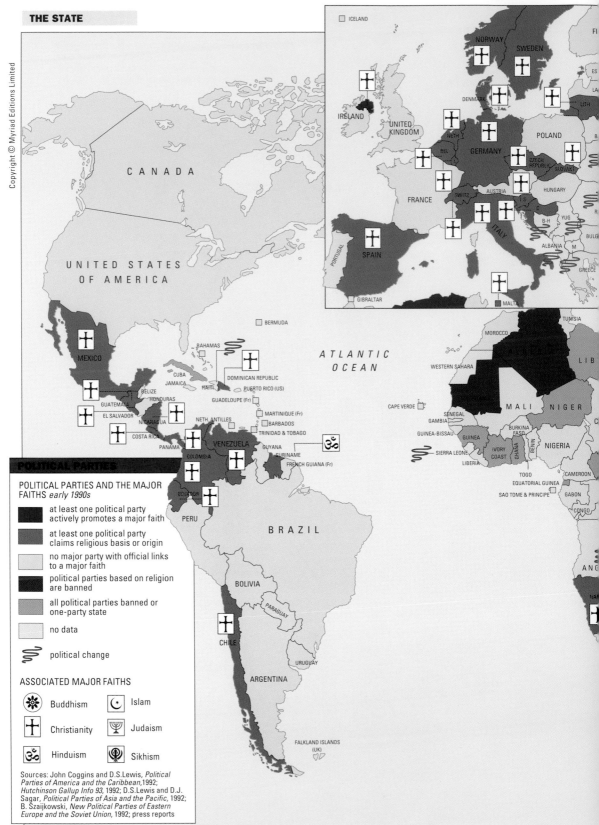

POLITICAL PARTIES

POLITICAL PARTIES AND THE MAJOR
FAITHS *early 1990s*

- at least one political party
  actively promotes a major faith
- at least one political party
  claims religious basis or origin
- no major party with official links
  to a major faith
- political parties based on religion
  are banned
- all political parties banned or
  one-party state
- no data

- political change

ASSOCIATED MAJOR FAITHS

- Buddhism
- Christianity
- Hinduism
- Islam
- Judaism
- Sikhism

Sources: John Coggins and D.S.Lewis, *Political
Parties of America and the Caribbean*,1992;
Hutchinson Gallup Info 93, 1992; D.S.Lewis and D.J.
Sagar, *Political Parties of Asia and the Pacific*, 1992;
B. Szaijkowski, *New Political Parties of Eastern
Europe and the Soviet Union*, 1992; press reports

Religion and politics do not mix, say many politicians across the political spectrum. But many parties have religious origins or links.

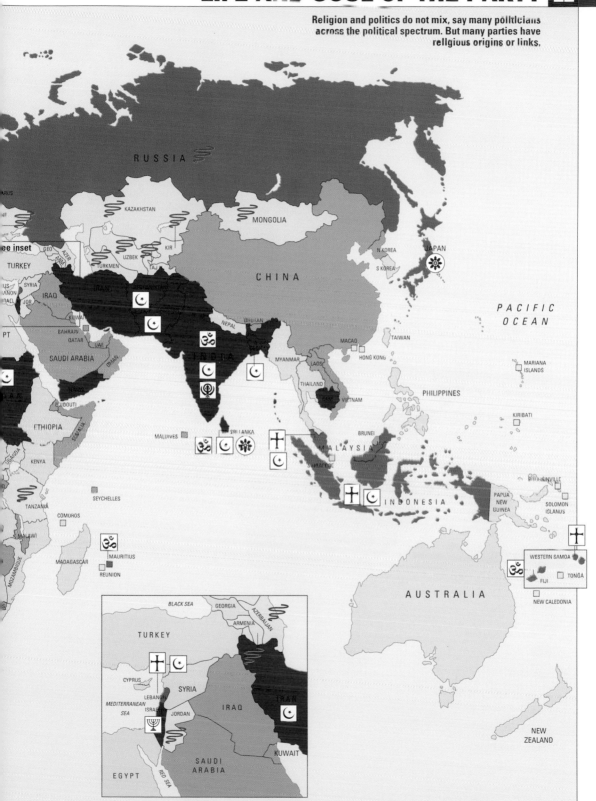

RUSSIA

KAZAKHSTAN

MONGOLIA

JAPAN

KIR

UZBEK

TURKMEN

TAJ

CHINA

N KOREA

S KOREA

ee inset

GEO

AZER

ARM

TURKEY

SYRIA

LEBANON

ISRAEL

IRAQ

JOR

KUWAIT

BAHRAIN

QATAR

UAE

SAUDI ARABIA

OMAN

ERITREA

DJIBOUTI

ETHIOPIA

UGANDA

KENYA

TANZANIA

COMOROS

MALAWI

MOZAMBIQUE

MADAGASCAR

REUNION

MAURITIUS

SEYCHELLES

MALDIVES

INDIA

NEPAL

BHUTAN

MYANMAR

LAOS

THAILAND

VIETNAM

SRI LANKA

MACAO

TAIWAN

HONG KONG

PHILIPPINES

MARIANA ISLANDS

KIRIBATI

MALAYSIA

SINGAPORE

BRUNEI

INDONESIA

PAPUA NEW GUINEA

BOUGAINVILLE

SOLOMON ISLANDS

NEW CALEDONIA

WESTERN SAMOA

FIJI

TONGA

AUSTRALIA

NEW ZEALAND

PACIFIC OCEAN

BLACK SEA

GEORGIA

ARMENIA

AZERBAIJAN

TURKEY

CYPRUS

SYRIA

LEBANON

MEDITERRANEAN SEA

ISRAEL

JORDAN

IRAQ

IRAN

KUWAIT

SAUDI ARABIA

EGYPT

RED SEA

Copyright © Myriad Editions Limited

ICELAND

NORWAY
SWEDEN
FI
DENMARK
LATVIA
IRELAND
?!
UNITED
KINGDOM
NETH
SEL
GERMANY
?!
POLAND
FRANCE
CZECH
REPUBLIC
SLOVAK
U
SWITZ
AUSTRIA
HUNGARY
S
ROMAN
PORTUGAL
SPAIN
C
B-H
YUG
BULG
ITALY
ALBANIA
M
GREECE
MALTA

CANADA

UNITED STATES
OF AMERICA
?!

BERMUDA

MEXICO

ATLANTIC
OCEAN

TUNISIA

WESTERN SAHARA

BAHAMAS

CUBA
DOMINICAN REPUBLIC
HAITI
PUERTO RICO (US)
JAMAICA
BELIZE
HONDURAS
GUATEMALA
GUADELOUPE (Fr)
EL SALVADOR
MARTINIQUE (Fr)
NICARAGUA
NETH. ANTILLES
BARBADOS
COSTA RICA
TRINIDAD & TOBAGO
PANAMA
VENEZUELA
GUYANA
SURINAME
FRENCH GUIANA (Fr)
COLOMBIA

CAPE VERDE

MALI
NIGER

SENEGAL
GAMBIA
BURKINA
FASO
GUINEA-BISSAU
GUINEA
SIERRA LEONE
IVORY
COAST
GHANA
BENIN
NIGERIA
LIBERIA
TOGO
EQUATORIAL GUINEA
CAMEROON
SAO TOME & PRINCIPE
GABON
CONGO

PACIFIC
OCEAN

ECUADOR

PERU

BRAZIL

ANG

BOLIVIA

NAM

CHILE

URUGUAY

ARGENTINA

FALKLAND ISLANDS
(UK)

RELIGIOUS EDUCATION

RELIGIOUS EDUCATION IN
STATE SCHOOLS *1993*

- single faith
- multi-faith with emphasis
  on majority faith
- multi-faith
- religious education optional
- no religious education
- political change leading
  to more religious education

?! religious education
under debate

no data

Sources: D.B. Barrett, ed. *World Christian
Encyclopedia,* 1982; *British Journal of
Religious Education;* World Council of
Churches

As societies become multi-cultural, religious education
is moving away from one of its major roles, of
indoctrination into the majority faith.

RUSSIA

KAZAKHSTAN

MONGOLIA

TURKEY

GEO AZER
ARM
TURKMEN UZBEK KIR
TAJ

N.KOREA JAPAN

S.KOREA

CHINA

SYRIA
ANON
RAEL JOR
IRAQ IRAN
AFGHANISTAN
PAKISTAN

BHUTAN

PACIFIC
OCEAN

KUWAIT
BAHRAIN
QATAR

SAUDI ARABIA

YEMEN

DJIBOUTI

ETHIOPIA

NEPAL

INDIA

BDESH

MYANMAR

LAOS

THAILAND

CAM VIETNAM

MACAO TAIWAN

HONG KONG

PHILIPPINES

MARIANA
ISLANDS

KIRIBATI

MALDIVES

SRI LANKA

BRUNEI

MALAYSIA

SINGAPORE

KENYA

SEYCHELLES

TANZANIA

COMOROS

MALAWI

MADAGASCAR

MAURITIUS

REUNION

INDONESIA

PAPUA
NEW
GUINEA

SOLOMON
ISLANDS

WESTERN SAMOA

FIJI TONGA

NEW CALEDONIA

AUSTRALIA

MOZAMBIQUE

NEW
ZEALAND

Copyright © Myriad Editions Limited

ICELAND □ all recognized religions

NORWAY

FI

SWEDEN

all Christians, most to Lutherans

Christianity

Lutheran Orthodox Christian

ES

LITH

IRELAND

UNITED KINGDOM

Catholics, Protestants, Anglicans, Jews, Muslims

Christianity DENMARK

NETH

BEL

Catholics, Protestants

GERMANY

POLAND

CZECH REPUBLIC

SLOVAK

FRANCE

AUSTRIA

HUNGARY

ROMA

SWITZ

S

B-H

YUG

BULG

Christianity

ITALY

ALBANIA

M

Christianity
SPAIN

PORTUGAL

Christianity

GREECE

Christiani

MALTA □

CANADA

UNITED STATES OF AMERICA

BERMUDA □

ATLANTIC OCEAN

TUNISIA

MOROCCO

ALGERIA

LIB

MEXICO

BAHAMAS □

CUBA

Christianity
DOMINICAN REPUBLIC

HAITI

JAMAICA

PUERTO RICO (US)

WESTERN SAHARA

BELIZE

HONDURAS

GUATEMALA

EL SALVADOR

NICARAGUA

COSTA RICA

PANAMA

BARBADOS □

TRINIDAD & TOBAGO

VENEZUELA

GUYANA

SURINAME

FRENCH GUIANA (Fr)

CAPE VERDE □

MAURITANIA

MALI

NIGER

SENEGAL

GAMBIA

GUINEA-BISSAU

GUINEA

SIERRA LEONE

IVORY COAST

BURKINA FASO

GHANA

BENIN

NIGERIA

LIBERIA

PACIFIC OCEAN

Christianity

COLOMBIA

all Christians

BRAZIL

ECUADOR

PERU

TOGO

EQUATORIAL GUINEA

SAO TOME & PRINCIPE

CAMEROON

GABON

CONGO

AN

BOLIVIA

PARAGUAY

AN

NA

CHILE

URUGUAY

ARGENTINA

FALKLAND ISLANDS (UK)

62

Substantial state funding, where given, goes usually to the majority faith. All states give at least minimal support: to religious charitable work, or to religious sites of national historical significance.

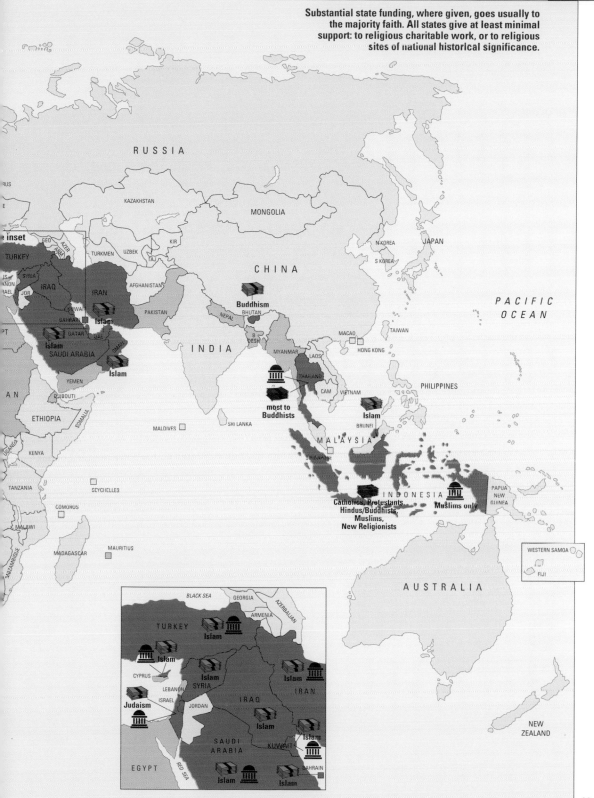

Copyright © Myriad Editions Limited

GREENLAND
(Den)

SVALBARD &
JA N MAYEN ISLANDS

FAROE ISLANDS

ICELAND

NORWAY
SWEDEN

C A N A D A

IRELAND
UNITED
KINGDOM

DENMARK

NETH
BEL
GERMANY
CZ
AUS

FRANCE
MONACO
S
ITALY

UNITED STATES
OF AMERICA

ANDORRA
HOLY SEE

PORTUGAL
SPAIN

GIBRALTAR (UK)
TUNISIA
MALT

BERMUDA

MEXICO

BAHAMAS

CUBA
HAITI
DOMINICAN REPUBLIC
PUERTO RICO (US)

BELIZE
GUATEMALA
HONDURAS
JAMAICA
GUADELOUPE (Fr)

EL SALVADOR
NICARAGUA
NETH. ANTILLES
GRENADA
MARTINIQUE (Fr)
BARBADOS

COSTA RICA
TRINIDAD & TOBAGO

PANAMA
VENEZUELA
GUYANA

COLOMBIA
SURINAME
FRENCH GUIANA (Fr)

ECUADOR

PERU

BRAZIL

A T L A N T I C
O C E A N

CAPE VERDE

P A C I F I C
O C E A N

MOROCCO

WESTERN SAHARA

A L G E R I A

unique
Libyan soc

MAURITANIA

M A L I

N I G E R

SENEGAL
GAMBIA
GUINEA-BISSAU
GUINEA
BURKINA
FASO
BENIN
NIGERIA

SIERRA LEONE
IVORY
COAST
GHANA

LIBERIA

TOGO
CAMEROON

EQUATORIAL GUINEA
SAO TOME & PRINCIPE
GABON

CONGO

A N

N A

BOLIVIA

PARAGUAY

CHILE

URUGUAY

ARGENTINA

FALKLAND ISLANDS
(UK)

THE SHARI'AH

THE LEGAL SYSTEM AND COURTS
IN MUSLIM MAJORITY STATES *1993*

- Islamic law only:
  based on the Shari'ah
- in transition to Islamic law
- combination of Islamic and
  secular law
- Islamic law and secular law
  exist side by side
- secular law only
- gambling and alcohol
  forbidden
- non-Muslim states

Sources: Mawil Izzi-Dien; C. Horrie and
P. Chippindale, *What is Islam?* 1990;
F. Shaikh, ed. *Islam and Islamic Groups*, 1992.

The Shari'ah sets out for Muslims the basic codes, legal
and ethical, upon which all relationships and institutions
should be founded and by which they should be guided.

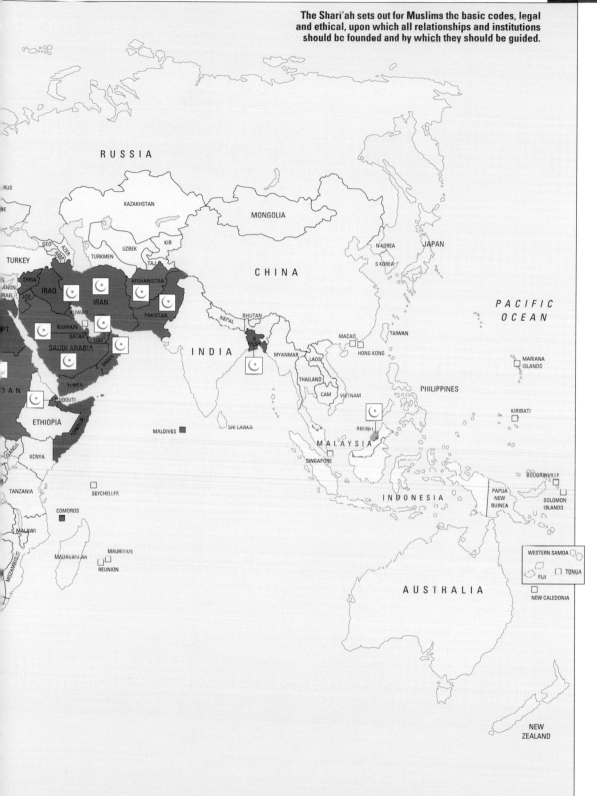

RUSSIA

KAZAKHSTAN

MONGOLIA

CYPRUS

GEO
ARM AZER

TURKEY

TURKMEN

UZBEK

KIR

TAJ

N KOREA

JAPAN

S KOREA

CHINA

PACIFIC
OCEAN

SYRIA
LEBANON
ISRAEL
JOR

IRAQ

KUWAIT

IRAN

AFGHANISTAN

PAKISTAN

NEPAL

BHUTAN

BAHRAIN
QATAR
UAE

OMAN

MACAO

TAIWAN

HONG KONG

MARIANA
ISLANDS

EGYPT

SAUDI ARABIA

INDIA

BANGLADESH

MYANMAR

LAOS

YEMEN

THAILAND

CAM

VIETNAM

PHILIPPINES

KIRIBATI

SUDAN

DJIBOUTI

SOMALIA

ETHIOPIA

MALDIVES

SRI LANKA

BRUNEI

KENYA

MALAYSIA

UGANDA

SINGAPORE

INDONESIA

BOUGAINVILLE

TANZANIA

SEYCHELLES

PAPUA
NEW
GUINEA

SOLOMON
ISLANDS

MALAWI

COMOROS

MOZAMBIQUE

MADAGASCAR

MAURITIUS

REUNION

AUSTRALIA

WESTERN SAMOA

FIJI

TONGA

NEW CALEDONIA

NEW
ZEALAND

ICELAND

NORWAY

SWEDEN

FI

ES

DENMARK

LA

LITH

NORTHERN
IRELAND

Belfast
Christian/
Christian

IRELAND

UNITED
KINGDOM

NETH

BEL

GERMANY

POLAND

CZECH
REPUBLIC

SLOVAKIA

FRANCE

AUSTRIA

SWITZ

SLO

HUNGARY

ROMA

ITALY

CROATIA

BOSNIA

Christia
Muslim
Christia

Sarajevo

SERBIA

BUL

form
YUG

ALBANIA

GREECE

PORTUGAL

SPAIN

GIBRALTAR

MALTA

C A N A D A

U N I T E D   S T A T E S
O F   A M E R I C A

MEXICO

BERMUDA

A T L A N T I C
O C E A N

BAHAMAS

CUBA

DOMINICAN REPUBLIC

HAITI

PUERTO RICO (US)

BELIZE

JAMAICA

GUADELOUPE (Fr)

HONDURAS

GUATEMALA

EL SALVADOR

NICARAGUA

NETH. ANTILLES

GRENADA

MARTINIQUE (Fr)

BARBADOS

COSTA RICA

TRINIDAD & TOBAGO

PANAMA

VENEZUELA

GUYANA

SURINAME

FRENCH GUIANA (Fr)

P A C I F I C
O C E A N

COLOMBIA

ECUADOR

B R A Z I L

PERU

BOLIVIA

PARAGUAY

CHILE

URUGUAY

ARGENTINA

FALKLAND ISLANDS
(UK)

TUNISIA

MOROCCO

ALGERIA

LIB

WESTERN SAHARA

MAURITANIA

MALI

NIGER

CAPE VERDE

SENEGAL

GAMBIA

GUINEA-BISSAU

GUINEA

BURKINA
FASO

NIGERIA

SIERRA LEONE

IVORY
COAST

GHANA

BENIN

LIBERIA

TOGO

CAMEROON

EQUATORIAL GUINEA

GABON

SAO TOME & PRINCIPE

CONGO

AN

NA

FAITH AT WAR

**WARS WITH SOME RELIGIOUS
INVOLVEMENT** *January 1993*

- war with foreign state
- general civil war
- regional civil war
- other states

Religion directly involved

- conflict to enforce strict
religious law

- conflict to achieve independent
religious/ethnic state

**Religion is one factor, along with
territorial, political and ethnic issues**

- a significant factor
- a factor
- a minor factor

Sources: M. Kidron & D. Smith, *The New State
of War and Peace: An International Atlas*, 1991;
Ecumenical Press Service, WCC; press reports

Most religions preach peace, yet the catalogue of wars in the name of religion down the ages seems to belie the claim. In the wars of the early 1990s, religion is rarely the major factor but its role is increasing.

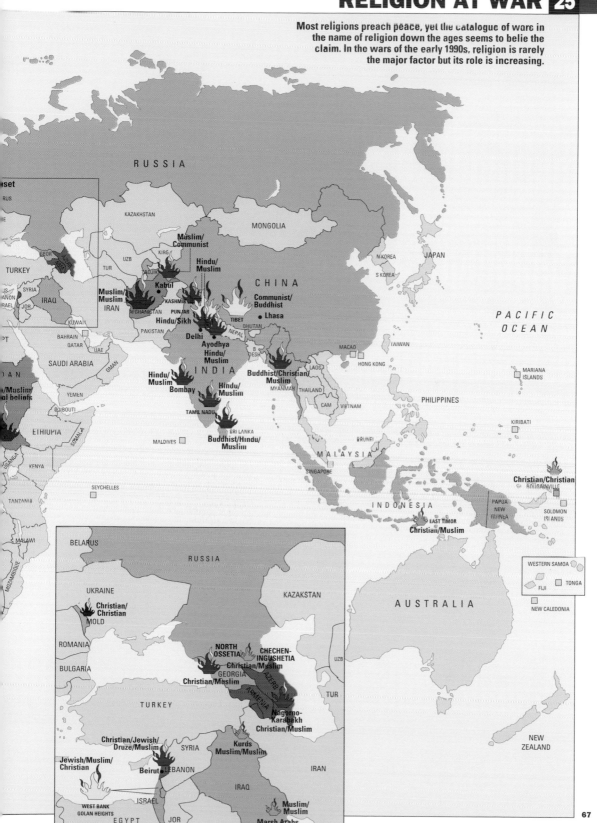

RUSSIA

KAZAKHSTAN

MONGOLIA

N.KOREA
JAPAN

S.KOREA

CHINA

**Muslim/
Communist**

**Hindu/
Muslim**

Kabul

KASHMIR

**Muslim/
Muslim**

IRAN

AFGHANISTAN

PUNJAB

**Communist/
Buddhist**

TIBET

• Lhasa

PAKISTAN

Hindu/Sikh

Delhi

BHUTAN

NEPAL

B
DESH

MACAO

TAIWAN

PACIFIC
OCEAN

BAHRAIN

QATAR

UAE

OMAN

SAUDI ARABIA

YEMEN

DJIBOUTI

**Ayodhya
Hindu/
Muslim**

INDIA

**Hindu/
Muslim**

Bombay

**Hindu/
Muslim**

**Buddhist/Christian/
Muslim**

MYANMAR

THAILAND

LAOS

HONG KONG

PHILIPPINES

MARIANA
ISLANDS

TURKEY

SYRIA

IRAQ

KUWAIT

IS
ANON
RAEL
JOR

GEOR

ARM

AZERB

TUR

UZB

KIRG

TAJIK

KIRIBATI

TAMIL NADU

SRI LANKA

**Buddhist/Hindu/
Muslim**

MALDIVES

CAM

VIETNAM

BRUNEI

**/Muslim/
al beliefs**

ETHIOPIA

SOMALIA

UGANDA

KENYA

MALAWI

TANZANIA

SEYCHELLES

SINGAPORE

MALAYSIA

INDONESIA

Christian/Christian
BOUGAINVILLE

PAPUA
NEW
GUINEA

SOLOMON
ISLANDS

EAST TIMOR
Christian/Muslim

AUSTRALIA

WESTERN SAMOA

FIJI

TONGA

NEW CALEDONIA

NEW
ZEALAND

BELARUS

RUSSIA

UKRAINE

KAZAKSTAN

**Christian/
Christian**
MOLD

ROMANIA

BULGARIA

GEORGIA

**NORTH
OSSETIA**

**CHECHEN-
INGUSHETIA**

Christian/Muslim

Christian/Muslim

ARMENIA

AZERB

UZB

TUR

TURKEY

**Christian/Jewish/
Druze/Muslim**

SYRIA

**Kurds
Muslim/Muslim**

**Nagorno-
Karabakh
Christian/Muslim**

**Jewish/Muslim/
Christian**

Beirut

LEBANON

IRAN

ISRAEL

IRAQ

WEST BANK
GOLAN HEIGHTS

EGYPT

JOR

**Muslim/
Muslim**

Marsh Arabs

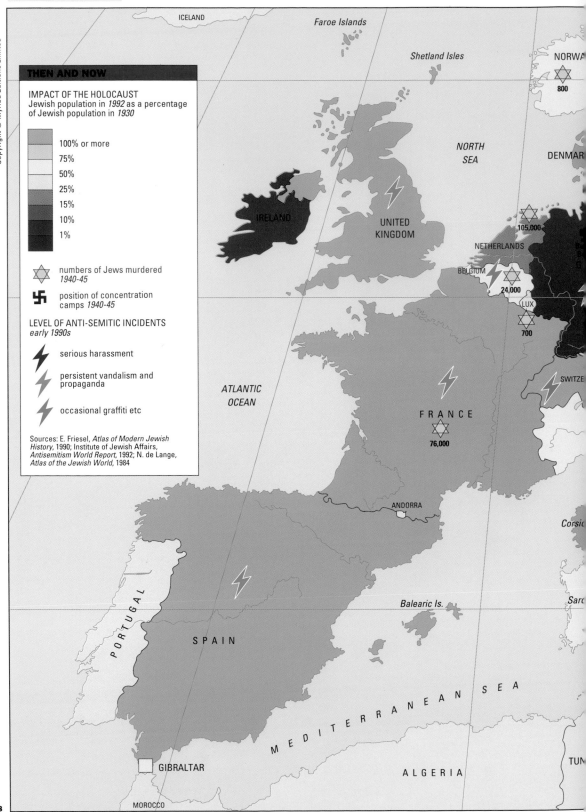

Copyright © Myriad Editions Limited

THEN AND NOW

IMPACT OF THE HOLOCAUST
Jewish population in *1992* as a percentage
of Jewish population in *1930*

- 100% or more
- 75%
- 50%
- 25%
- 15%
- 10%
- 1%

✡ numbers of Jews murdered
1940-45

卐 position of concentration
camps *1940-45*

LEVEL OF ANTI-SEMITIC INCIDENTS
early 1990s

⚡ serious harassment

⚡ persistent vandalism and
propaganda

⚡ occasional graffiti etc

Sources: E. Friesel, *Atlas of Modern Jewish
History*, 1990; Institute of Jewish Affairs,
Antisemitism World Report, 1992; N. de Lange,
Atlas of the Jewish World, 1984

ICELAND

Faroe Islands

Shetland Isles

NORWA

NORTH
SEA

DENMAR

IRELAND

UNITED
KINGDOM

NETHERLANDS

✡ 105,000

BELGIUM

✡ 24,000

LUX

✡ 700

ATLANTIC
OCEAN

SWITZE

FRANCE

✡ 76,000

ANDORRA

Corsic

PORTUGAL

Balearic Is.

Sar

SPAIN

M E D I T E R R A N E A N   S E A

GIBRALTAR

ALGERIA

TUN

MOROCCO

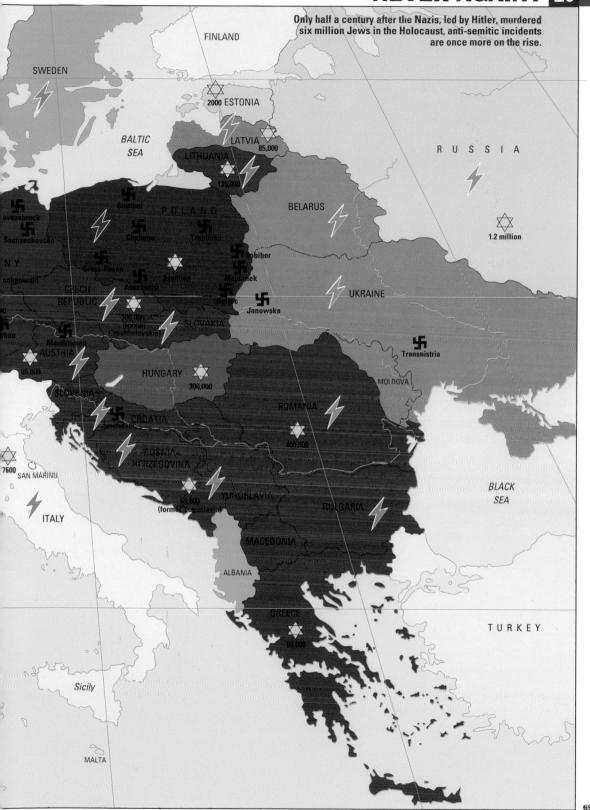

Only half a century after the Nazis, led by Hitler, murdered six million Jews in the Holocaust, anti-semitic incidents are once more on the rise.

FINLAND

SWEDEN

2000 ESTONIA

BALTIC SEA

LATVIA
85,000

LITHUANIA
135,000

RUSSIA

POLAND

BELARUS

1.2 million

Stutthof

Chelmno

Treblinka

Sobibor

Gross-Rosen

2 million

Majdanek

Auschwitz

Belzec

Janowska

UKRAINE

CZECH REPUBLIC

Buchenwald

N Y

300,000 (former Czechoslovakia)

Theresienstadt

SLOVAKIA

Mauthausen

AUSTRIA
65,000

HUNGARY
300,000

Transnistria

MOLDOVA

SLOVENIA

CROATIA
Jasenovac

BOSNIA HERZEGOVINA

ROMANIA
400,000

7500
SAN MARINO

ITALY

85,000 (former Yugoslavia)

YUGOSLAVIA

BULGARIA

BLACK SEA

MACEDONIA

ALBANIA

GREECE
60,000

TURKEY

Sicily

MALTA

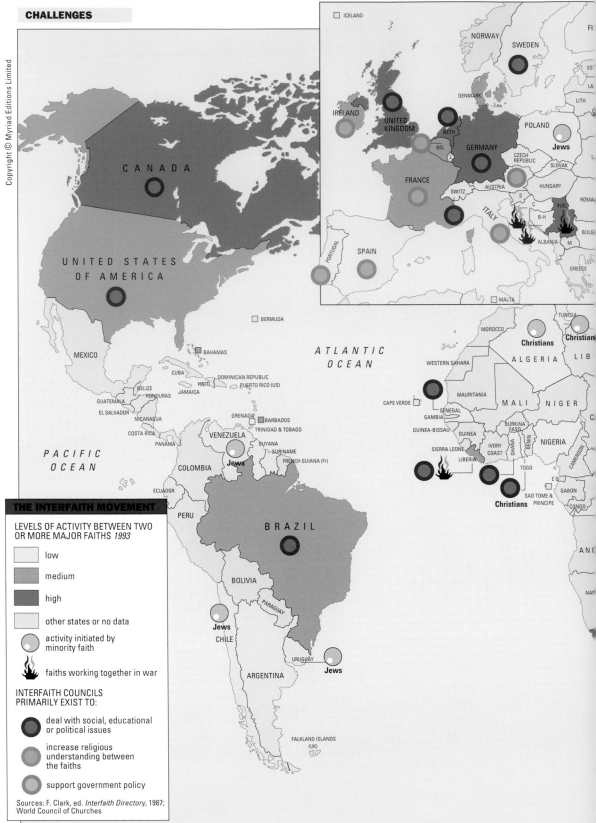

Copyright © Myriad Editions Limited

THE INTERFAITH MOVEMENT

LEVELS OF ACTIVITY BETWEEN TWO OR MORE MAJOR FAITHS *1993*

- low
- medium
- high
- other states or no data
- activity initiated by minority faith
- faiths working together in war

INTERFAITH COUNCILS PRIMARILY EXIST TO:

- deal with social, educational or political issues
- increase religious understanding between the faiths
- support government policy

Sources: F. Clark, ed. *Interfaith Directory*, 1987; World Council of Churches

After a century of effort the interfaith movement is still
limited. Religions sometimes work together over social
or political problems. Often, minority faiths seek to form
links which will give them recognition.

Copyright © Myriad Editions Limited

ICELAND

NORWAY SWEDEN FI

ES

DENMARK LITH

IRELAND

UNITED
KINGDOM NETH POLAND

BEL GERMANY CZECH
REPUBLIC SLOVAK

FRANCE SWITZ AUSTRIA HUNGARY ROMAN

ITALY S C BULG

B-H YUG M

ALBANIA

PORTUGAL SPAIN GREECE

GIBRALTAR MALTA

C A N A D A

UNITED STATES
OF AMERICA

BERMUDA

A T L A N T I C
O C E A N

TUNISIA

MOROCCO

ALGERIA LIB

WESTERN SAHARA

BAHAMAS

CUBA MAURITANIA MALI NIGER

MEXICO DOMINICAN REPUBLIC
HAITI PUERTO RICO (US)

BELIZE JAMAICA GUADELOUPE (Fr) CAPE VERDE

HONDURAS SENEGAL

GUATEMALA MARTINIQUE (Fr) GAMBIA BURKINA
FASO

EL SALVADOR NETH. ANTILLES GRENADA BARBADOS GUINEA-BISSAU

NICARAGUA TRINIDAD & TOBAGO GUINEA BENIN NIGERIA

COSTA RICA SIERRA LEONE IVORY GHANA CAMEROON
COAST

PANAMA VENEZUELA GUYANA LIBERIA TOGO

P A C I F I C
O C E A N SURINAME EQUATORIAL GUINEA

COLOMBIA FRENCH GUIANA (Fr) GABON

ECUADOR SAO TOME & CONGO
PRINCIPE

PERU ANG

B R A Z I L NAM

BOLIVIA

PARAGUAY

CHILE

URUGUAY

ARGENTINA

FALKLAND ISLANDS
(UK)

TIE AND TEAR

UNITY AND TENSIONS WITHIN NATIONAL
CHRISTIAN COMMUNITIES IN RECENT
DECADES

significant steps have been
taken towards unity or
reunion

increase in tensions or new
divisions or denominations

no major developments

Sources: Ecumenical Press Service;
World Council of Churches; press reports

There has been a drive towards a united Christian church since the beginning of the century. There have been some reunion schemes, notably in non-Christian majority countries, but there are now more Christian denominations than ever.

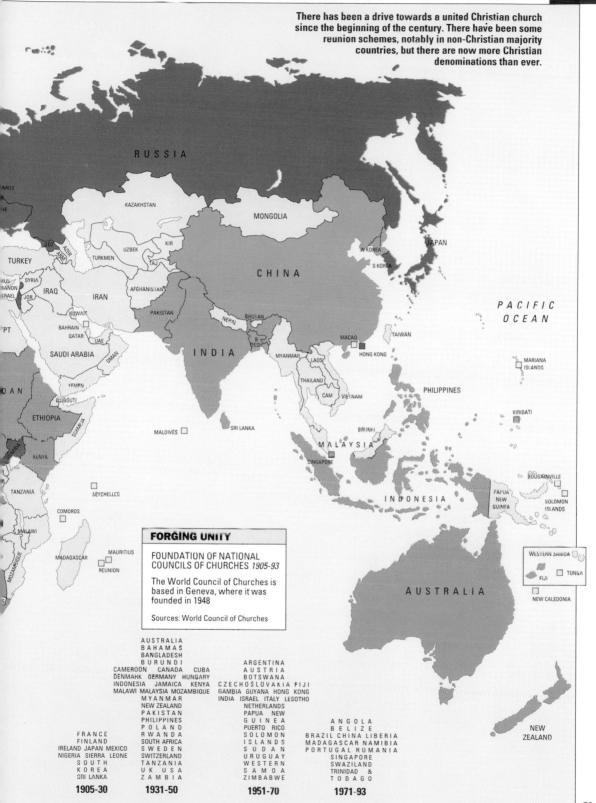

FORGING UNITY

FOUNDATION OF NATIONAL COUNCILS OF CHURCHES *1905-93*

The World Council of Churches is based in Geneva, where it was founded in 1948

Sources: World Council of Churches

1905-30	1931-50	1951-70	1971-93
	AUSTRALIA		
	BAHAMAS		
	BANGLADESH		
	BURUNDI	ARGENTINA	
	CAMEROON CANADA CUBA	AUSTRIA	
	DENMARK GERMANY HUNGARY	BOTSWANA	
	INDONESIA JAMAICA KENYA	CZECHOSLOVAKIA FIJI	
	MALAWI MALAYSIA MOZAMBIQUE	GAMBIA GUYANA HONG KONG	
	MYANMAR	INDIA ISRAEL ITALY LESOTHO	
	NEW ZEALAND	NETHERLANDS	
	PAKISTAN	PAPUA NEW	
	PHILIPPINES	GUINEA	ANGOLA
	POLAND	PUERTO RICO	BELIZE
FRANCE	RWANDA	SOLOMON	BRAZIL CHINA LIBERIA
FINLAND	SOUTH AFRICA	ISLANDS	MADAGASCAR NAMIBIA
IRELAND JAPAN MEXICO	SWEDEN	SUDAN	PORTUGAL ROMANIA
NIGERIA SIERRA LEONE	SWITZERLAND	URUGUAY	SINGAPORE
SOUTH	TANZANIA	WESTERN	SWAZILAND
KOREA	UK USA	SAMOA	TRINIDAD &
SRI LANKA	ZAMBIA	ZIMBABWE	TOBAGO

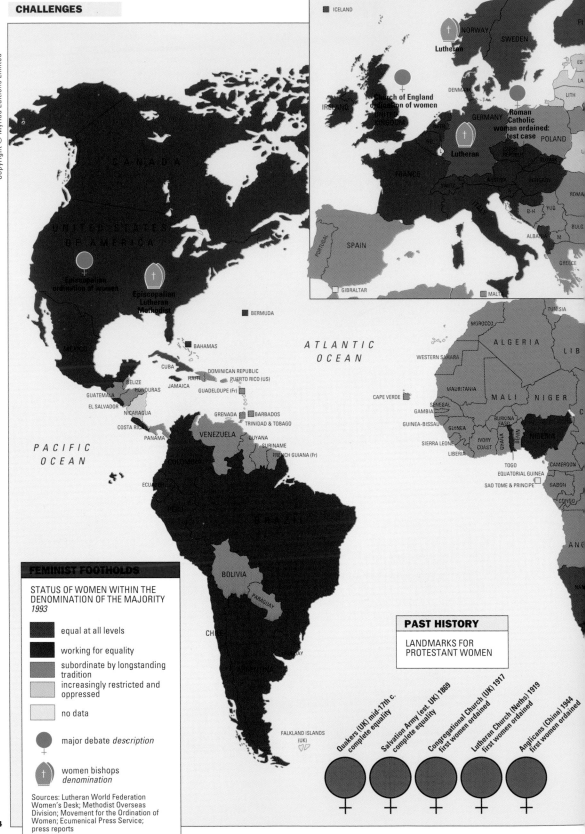

ICELAND

NORWAY
Lutheran
SWEDEN

DENMARK

Church of England
ordination of women
UNITED
KINGDOM
IRELAND

GERMANY
**Roman
Catholic
woman ordained:
test case**
POLAND

FRANCE

Lutheran

AUSTRIA
HUNGARY

SPAIN
PORTUGAL

ITALY

B-H   YUG

ALBANIA

GREECE

GIBRALTAR

MALTA

C A N A D A

U N I T E D S T A T E S
O F A M E R I C A

**Episcopalian
ordination of women**

**Episcopalian
Lutheran
Methodist**

MEXICO

BERMUDA

ATLANTIC
OCEAN

BAHAMAS

CUBA
HAITI   DOMINICAN REPUBLIC
BELIZE   JAMAICA   PUERTO RICO (US)
GUATEMALA   HONDURAS   GUADELOUPE (Fr)
EL SALVADOR
NICARAGUA   GRENADA   BARBADOS
COSTA RICA   TRINIDAD & TOBAGO
PANAMA   VENEZUELA
COLOMBIA   GUYANA
SURINAME
ECUADOR   FRENCH GUIANA (Fr)

PERU

B R A Z I L

BOLIVIA

PARAGUAY

CHILE

URUGUAY

ARGENTINA

FALKLAND ISLANDS
(UK)

PACIFIC
OCEAN

MOROCCO   TUNISIA
ALGERIA   LIB

WESTERN SAHARA

MAURITANIA   MALI   NIGER   C

CAPE VERDE   SENEGAL
GAMBIA
GUINEA-BISSAU   GUINEA   BURKINA
FASO
SIERRA LEONE   IVORY   GHANA   BENIN   NIGERIA
COAST
LIBERIA   TOGO   CAMEROON
EQUATORIAL GUINEA
SAO TOME & PRINCIPE   GABON   CONGO

ANG

NAM

FEMINIST FOOTHOLDS

STATUS OF WOMEN WITHIN THE
DENOMINATION OF THE MAJORITY
1993

equal at all levels

working for equality

subordinate by longstanding
tradition

increasingly restricted and
oppressed

no data

major debate *description*

women bishops
denomination

Sources: Lutheran World Federation
Women's Desk; Methodist Overseas
Division; Movement for the Ordination of
Women; Ecumenical Press Service;
press reports

PAST HISTORY

LANDMARKS FOR
PROTESTANT WOMEN

Quakers (UK) mid-17th c.
complete equality

Salvation Army (est. UK) 1869
complete equality

Congregational Church (UK) 1917
first women ordained

Lutheran Church (Neths) 1919
first women ordained

Anglicans (China) 1944
first women ordained

The women's movement has forced some religions to give women equal status and rights. Other religions claim that feminism is a `Western' issue and irrelevant to their faith.

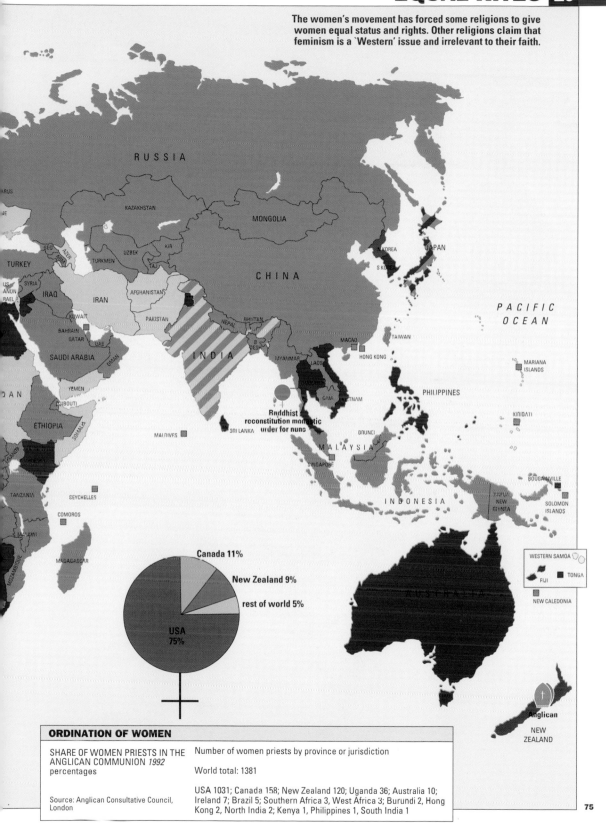

RUSSIA

KAZAKHSTAN

MONGOLIA

UZBEK

TURKMEN

KIR

TAJ

CHINA

N.KOREA

JAPAN

S.KOREA

TURKEY

AZER

GEO

ARM

US
ANON
RAEL'T

SYRIA

IRAQ

IRAN

AFGHANISTAN

PAKISTAN

NEPAL

BHUTAN

B
DESH

PACIFIC
OCEAN

KUWAIT

BAHRAIN

QATAR

UAE

OMAN

SAUDI ARABIA

YEMEN

DJIBOUTI

DAN

ETHIOPIA

SOMALIA

INDIA

MYANMAR

LAOS

MACAO

TAIWAN

HONG KONG

MARIANA
ISLANDS

PHILIPPINES

CAM

VIETNAM

KIRIBATI

MALDIVES

SRI LANKA

Buddhist
reconstitution monastic
order for nuns

BRUNEI

MALAYSIA

SINGAPORE

SEYCHELLES

TANZANIA

COMOROS

MALAWI

MADAGASCAR

MOZAMBIQUE

INDONESIA

PAPUA
NEW
GUINEA

BOUGAINVILLE

SOLOMON
ISLANDS

Canada 11%

New Zealand 9%

rest of world 5%

USA
75%

AUSTRALIA

WESTERN SAMOA

FIJI

TONGA

NEW CALEDONIA

✝
Anglican

NEW
ZEALAND

ORDINATION OF WOMEN

SHARE OF WOMEN PRIESTS IN THE
ANGLICAN COMMUNION *1992*
percentages

Source: Anglican Consultative Council,
London

Number of women priests by province or jurisdiction

World total: 1381

USA 1031; Canada 158; New Zealand 120; Uganda 36; Australia 10;
Ireland 7; Brazil 5; Southern Africa 3; West Africa 3; Burundi 2; Hong
Kong 2; North India 2; Kenya 1; Philippines 1; South India 1

ICELAND

NORWAY
against acid rain

SWEDEN
against acid rain

against industrial pollution

DENMARK

IRELAND

UNITED KINGDOM

NETH
anti-nuclear against industrial pollution

BEL
against industrial pollution

LITH

organic farming against industrial pollution
POLAND

FRANCE

GERMANY

CZECH REPUBLIC

SLOVAK

AUSTRIA

SWITZ
anti-nuclear

HUNGARY

organic far against industria pollutio

SPAIN

S.

YUG

B-H

M

PORTUGAL
wildlife reserves

anti-nuclear against damming

ITALY

ALBANIA

BUL

GREECE

GIBRALTAR

MALTA

land management reforestation

C A N A D A
against land development

UNITED STATES
OF AMERICA

BERMUDA

TUNISIA

MOROCCO

ALGERIA

LIB

against toxic waste dumping
MEXICO

BAHAMAS

CUBA

HAITI

DOMINICAN REPUBLIC

PUERTO RICO (US)

A T L A N T I C
O C E A N

WESTERN SAHARA

BELIZE

JAMAICA

HONDURAS

GUATEMALA

EL SALVADOR

NICARAGUA

COSTA RICA

PANAMA

wildlife reserves

GRENADA

BARBADOS

TRINIDAD & TOBAGO

VENEZUELA

GUYANA

SURINAME

FRENCH GUIANA (Fr)

CAPE VERDE

MAURITANIA

MALI

SENEGAL

GAMBIA

GUINEA-BISSAU

GUINEA

SIERRA LEONE

LIBERIA

IVORY COAST

BURKINA FASO

GHANA

TOGO

BENIN

NIGER

NIGERIA

desert reclamation

CAMEROON

wildlife reserves

COLOMBIA

ECUADOR

PERU

B R A Z I L
against deforestation

P A C I F I C
O C E A N

BOLIVIA

PARAGUAY

CHILE

URUGUAY

ARGENTINA

FALKLAND ISLANDS
(UK)

land reclamation reforestation

EQUATORIAL GUINEA

SAO TOME & PRINCIPE

GABON

CONGO

A N

NA

GREEN FAITH

INVOLVEMENT OF RELIGIONS IN
ENVIRONMENTAL CAMPAIGNS

multi-faith involvement in high-profile
environmental campaigns

majority religion demonstrates practical
commitment to the environment:

worldwide

within own state

majority religion responds to
environmental crises only

no significant activity

no data

Buddhists

Christians

Hindus

Muslims

Jains

Jews

Indigenous
peoples

Sources: WWF International, Network on Conservation
and Religion, Geneva; Ecumenical Press Service

The environmental crisis has provoked the religions into a major re-examination of their basic teachings and beliefs. They are now taking significant action worldwide, often working together.

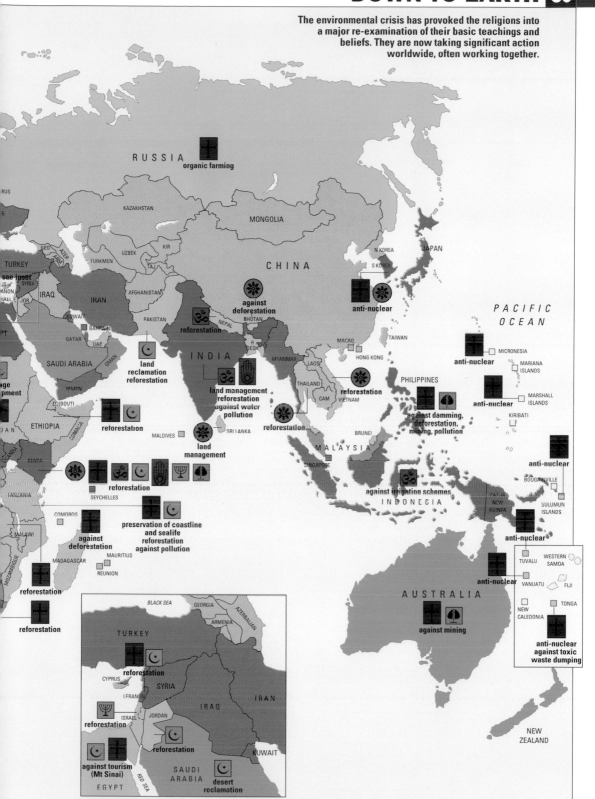

RUSSIA
organic farming

KAZAKHSTAN

MONGOLIA

TURKEY
see inset
SYRIA
IRAQ

N.KOREA
S.KOREA
JAPAN
anti-nuclear

CHINA
against deforestation

IRAN

AFGHANISTAN

PAKISTAN
NEPAL
reforestation
BHUTAN

PACIFIC OCEAN

TAIWAN

MACAO
HONG KONG

MICRONESIA
anti-nuclear
MARIANA ISLANDS

SAUDI ARABIA
land reclamation reforestation

INDIA
land management reforestation against water pollution

MYANMAR
LAOS
THAILAND
VIETNAM
CAM

reforestation

PHILIPPINES

anti-nuclear
MARSHALL ISLANDS

KIRIBATI

ETHIOPIA
reforestation

MALDIVES

SRI LANKA
reforestation

land management

reforestation

against damming, deforestation, mining, pollution

anti-nuclear

KENYA

SEYCHELLES
reforestation

BRUNEI

MALAYSIA

SINGAPORE

TANZANIA

COMOROS

preservation of coastline and sealife reforestation against pollution

against irrigation schemes

INDONESIA

BOUGAINVILLE

SOLOMON ISLANDS

anti-nuclear

MALAWI

against deforestation

MAURITIUS
REUNION

MADAGASCAR

PAPUA NEW GUINEA

anti-nuclear

MOZAMBIQUE
reforestation

reforestation

AUSTRALIA

against mining

anti-nuclear

TUVALU
WESTERN SAMOA
VANUATU
FIJI

NEW CALEDONIA
TONGA

anti-nuclear against toxic waste dumping

NEW ZEALAND

Inset

BLACK SEA
GEORGIA
ARMENIA
AZERBAIJAN

TURKEY
reforestation

CYPRUS
SYRIA

IRAN

I.FRANJI

IRAQ

ISRAEL
reforestation

JORDAN

reforestation

KUWAIT

against tourism (Mt Sinai)

SAUDI ARABIA
desert reclamation

EGYPT
RED SEA

ICELAND

NORWAY

SWEDEN

FI

DENMARK

EST

LITH

IRELAND

UNITED
KINGDOM

NETH

BEL

GERMANY

POLAND

FRANCE

CZECH
REPUBLIC

SLOVAK

SWITZ

AUSTRIA

HUNGARY

ROMA

S

C

B-H

YUG

BULG

ITALY

ALBANIA

M

PORTUGAL

SPAIN

GREECE

GIBRALTAR

MALTA

C A N A D A

U N I T E D   S T A T E S
O F   A M E R I C A

BERMUDA

A T L A N T I C
O C E A N

TUNISIA

MOROCCO

ALGERIA

LIB

WESTERN SAHARA

MEXICO

BAHAMAS

CUBA

DOMINICAN REPUBLIC

HAITI

PUERTO RICO (US)

BELIZE

JAMAICA

HONDURAS

GUATEMALA

EL SALVADOR

N'CARAGUA

COSTA RICA

PANAMA

BARBADOS

TRINIDAD & TOBAGO

VENEZUELA

GUYANA

SURINAME

FRENCH GUIANA (Fr)

COLOMBIA

ECUADOR

PERU

CAPE VERDE

MAURITANIA

M A L I

N I G E R

C

SENEGAL

GAMBIA

GUINEA-BISSAU

GUINEA

SIERRA LEONE

IVORY
COAST

BURKINA
FASO

GHANA

BENIN

TOGO

NIGERIA

CAMEROON

EQUATORIAL GUINEA

SAO TOME & PRINCIPE

GABON

CONGO

LIBERIA

AN

B R A Z I L

P A C I F I C
O C E A N

BOLIVIA

PARAGUAY

NAM

CHILE

URUGUAY

ARGENTINA

FALKLAND ISLANDS
(UK)

LEBANON

SYRIA

ISRAEL

JORDAN

There will be a worldwide increase in religious
allegiance, intensity and diversity. In some countries
this will lead to further religious tension.

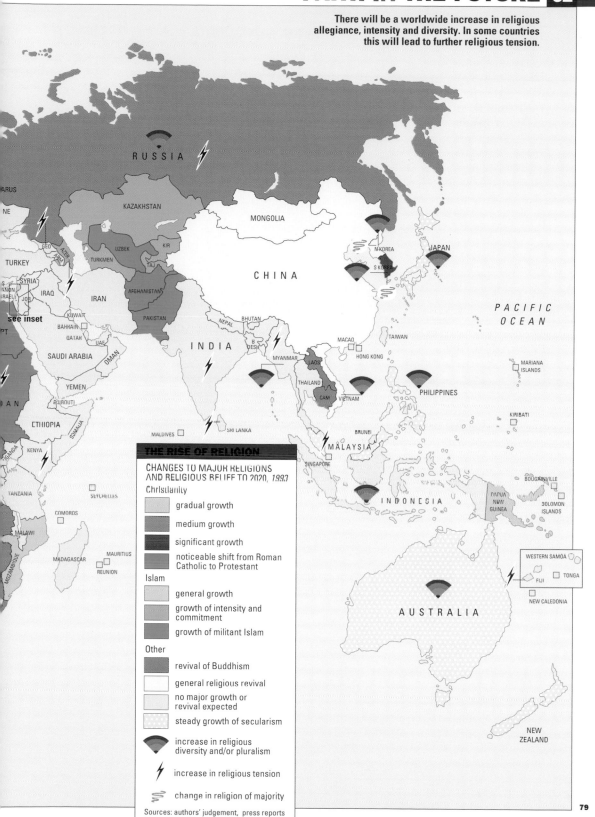

THE RISE OF RELIGION

CHANGES TO MAJOR RELIGIONS
AND RELIGIOUS BELIEF TO 2020, 1993

Christianity
- gradual growth
- medium growth
- significant growth
- noticeable shift from Roman
  Catholic to Protestant

Islam
- general growth
- growth of intensity and
  commitment
- growth of militant Islam

Other
- revival of Buddhism
- general religious revival
- no major growth or
  revival expected
- steady growth of secularism
- increase in religious
  diversity and/or pluralism
- increase in religious tension
- change in religion of majority

Sources: authors' judgement, press reports

Part 3

THE HEARTLANDS

Copyright © Myriad Editions Limited

ICELAND

NORWAY

SWEDEN

FIN

Presbyterianism 1560

Edinburgh

Anglicanism 1536

IRELAND

UNITED KINGDOM

ENGLAND

London

Bristol

Methodism 1795

Baptists 1609

Israel Jacobsen Reform and Liberal 1810

EST

LATV

DENMARK

LITH

Z. Frankel Conservative 1854

NETH

Amsterdam

Seesen

Martin Luther Protestantism and Lutheranism 1517

Wittenberg

BEL

GERMANY

Wrocław

POLAND

Baal Shem Tov Hassidim 1844

Mydzibo

B

UKRA

CZECH REPUBLIC

SLOVAK

FRANCE

Geneva

SWITZ

AUSTRIA

HUNGARY

ROMAN

John Calvin Calvinism 1541

ITALY

Rome

S

C

B-H

YUG

BULGA

ALBANIA

M

Roman Church 50 CE

GREECE

PORTUGAL

SPAIN

GIBRALTAR

MALTA

CANADA

UNITED STATES OF AMERICA

MEXICO

BERMUDA

BAHAMAS

CUBA

HAITI

DOMINICAN REPUBLIC

PUERTO RICO (US)

BELIZE

HONDURAS

JAMAICA

GUADELOUPE (Fr)

GUATEMALA

EL SALVADOR

NICARAGUA

NETH. ANTILLES

GRENADA

MARTINIQUE (Fr)

BARBADOS

TRINIDAD & TOBAGO

COSTA RICA

PANAMA

VENEZUELA

GUYANA

SURINAME

FRENCH GUIANA (Fr)

COLOMBIA

ECUADOR

PERU

BRAZIL

BOLIVIA

PARAGUAY

PACIFIC OCEAN

ATLANTIC OCEAN

TUNISIA

MOROCCO

ALGERIA

LIBY

WESTERN SAHARA

CAPE VERDE

MAURITANIA

MALI

NIGER

CH

SENEGAL

GAMBIA

GUINEA-BISSAU

GUINEA

BURKINA FASO

NIGERIA

SIERRA LEONE

IVORY COAST

GHANA

BENIN

LIBERIA

TOGO

CAMEROON

EQUATORIAL GUINEA

SAO TOME & PRINCIPE

GABON

CONGO

ANG

URUGUAY

ARGENTINA

CHILE

FALKLAND ISLANDS (UK)

NAM

ORIGINS

PLACES ASSOCIATED WITH THE ORIGINS OF THE MAJOR FAITHS *1993*
founders, leaders, places and dates

BCE Before Common Era (BC)

CE Common Era (AD)
not given after 1000CE

Buddhism

Jains

Christianity

Judaism

Confucianism

Sikhism

Islam

Taoism

PLACES ASSOCIATED WITH DIVISION OF THE MAJOR FAITHS
founders, places and dates where known

BCE Before Common Era (BC)

CE Common Era (AD)
not given after 1000CE

Buddhism

Christianity

Islam

Judaism

Taoism

Places associated with where the faiths began or where major new expressions came to life are often centres of pilgrimage and veneration.

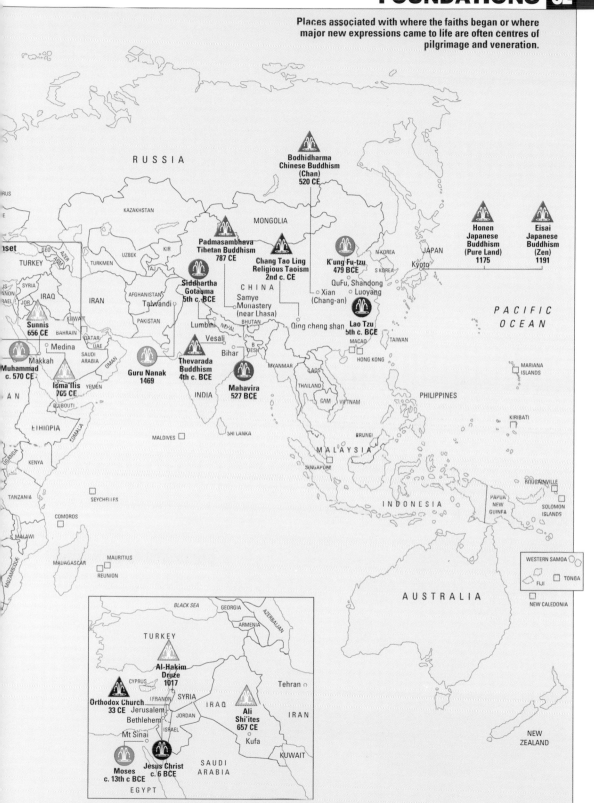

RUSSIA

Bodhidharma
Chinese Buddhism
(Chan)
520 CE

KAZAKHSTAN

MONGOLIA

Honen
Japanese
Buddhism
(Pure Land)
1175

Eisai
Japanese
Buddhism
(Zen)
1191

Padmasambhava
Tibetan Buddhism
787 CE

UZBEK   KIR

Chang Tao Ling
Religious Taoism
2nd c. CE

K'ung Fu-tzu
479 BCE

N-KOREA

JAPAN

S.KOREA

Kyoto

set

GEO

TURKEY

AZER
ARM

TURKMEN

TAJ

Siddhartha
Gotauma
5th c. BCE

CHINA

QuFu, Shandong

Xian
(Chang-an)

Luoyang

PACIFIC
OCEAN

S
ANON
RAEL

SYRIA
JOR

IRAQ

IRAN

AFGHANISTAN

Talwandi

Samye
Monastery
(near Lhasa)

PAKISTAN

BHUTAN

Qing cheng shan

Lao Tzu
5th c. BCE

TAIWAN

KUWAIT

BAHRAIN

Lumbini NEPAL

MACAO

Sunnis
656 CE

QATAR
UAE

Medina

SAUDI
ARABIA

OMAN

Vesali

Guru Nanak
1469

Bihar

B
DESH

MYANMAR

HONG KONG

MARIANA
ISLANDS

Muhammad
c. 570 CE

Makkah

Thevarada
Buddhism
4th c. BCE

LAOS

Isma'ilis
765 CE

YEMEN

N

DJIBOUTI

INDIA

Mahavira
527 BCE

THAILAND

VIETNAM
GAM

PHILIPPINES

KIRIBATI

ETHIOPIA

SOMALIA

MALDIVES

SRI LANKA

BRUNEI

MALAYSIA

BOUGAINVILLE

UGANDA

KENYA

SEYCHELLES

SINGAPORE

INDONESIA

PAPUA
NEW
GUINEA

SOLOMON
ISLANDS

TANZANIA

COMOROS

MADAGASCAR

MAURITIUS

REUNION

AUSTRALIA

WESTERN SAMOA

FIJI TONGA

MALAWI

MOZAMBIQUE

NEW CALEDONIA

BLACK SEA

GEORGIA

ARMENIA

AZERBAIJAN

TURKEY

Al-Hakim
Druze
1017

CYPRUS

I.FRANON

SYRIA

Tehran

Orthodox Church
33 CE Jerusalem

Bethlehem

IRAQ

JORDAN

ISRAEL

Ali
Shi'ites
657 CE

IRAN

Mt Sinai

Kufa

Moses
c. 13th c BCE

Jesus Christ
c. 6 BCE

SAUDI
ARABIA

KUWAIT

NEW
ZEALAND

EGYPT

Copyright © Myriad Editions Limited

ICELAND

NORWAY
SWEDEN

DENMARK

IRELAND
UNITED
KINGDOM

POLAND

NETH
GERMANY
BEL
CZECH
REPUBLIC
SLOVAK

FRANCE
AUSTRIA
HUNGARY

SWITZ
S
C
B-H
YUG

Santiago de
Compostela
Lourdes
ITALY
12th c.
Christian

Assisi

9th c. CE
Christian
19thc.
Christian
Rome
ALBANIA
M

SPAIN
PORTUGAL
2nd c. CE
Christian
GREECE

C A N A D A

Salt Lake City
19th c.
Mormon

UNITED STATES
OF AMERICA

BERMUDA

ATLANTIC
OCEAN

Chauen
Muslim
MOROCCO
Kairouan
Muslim
TUNISIA

ALGERIA
LIB

MEXICO

BAHAMAS

WESTERN SAHARA

CUBA
HAITI
DOMINICAN REPUBLIC
PUERTO RICO (US)

BELIZE
HONDURAS
JAMAICA
GUADELOUPE (Fr)

GUATEMALA
MARTINIQUE (Fr)
CAPE VERDE

MAURITANIA

MALI
NIGER

EL SALVADOR
NETH. ANTILLES
GRENADA
BARBADOS
SENEGAL
NICARAGUA
GAMBIA
BURKINA
FASO

COSTA RICA
TRINIDAD & TOBAGO
GUINEA-BISSAU
PANAMA
VENEZUELA
GUYANA
GUINEA
NIGERIA

PACIFIC
OCEAN
COLOMBIA
SURINAME
FRENCH GUIANA (Fr)
SIERRA LEONE
IVORY
COAST
GHANA
BENIN

LIBERIA

ECUADOR
TOGO
CAMEROON
EQUATORIAL GUINEA
PERU
BRAZIL
SAO TOME & PRINCIPE
GABON
CONGO

AN

BOLIVIA

NA

PARAGUAY

CHILE

URUGUAY

ARGENTINA

THE HAJJ

PLACE OF ORIGIN OF PILGRIMS
TO MAKKAH *1987*

total: 960,386 pilgrims

Sources: Saudi Information Office, London;
Kingdom of Saudi Arabia, Ministry of Finance
and National Economy, *Statistical Yearbook 1987*

non-Arab Asia
53%
non-Arab Africa
4%
Europe 0.7%
N. & S. America
0.2%
all Arab states
42%
Oceania
0.04%

URBAN PILGRIMAGE CENTRES

MAJOR CITIES AND TOWNS HOLY TO
ONE OR MORE WORLD RELIGION

Major tourist centres:

founded or built as a holy city
date

later became a holy city

other Holy cities or towns:

founded or built as holy
date

later became holy

site of religious tension

Sources: Aubrey Rose; Ranchor Prime; Iftikhar
Awan; Mawil Izzidien; Rupert Gethin

Holy cities often attract many tourists – religious and
non-religious. A few cities are holy to more than one
faith. Jerusalem is holy to three. Every Muslim will try to
visit Makkah at least once.

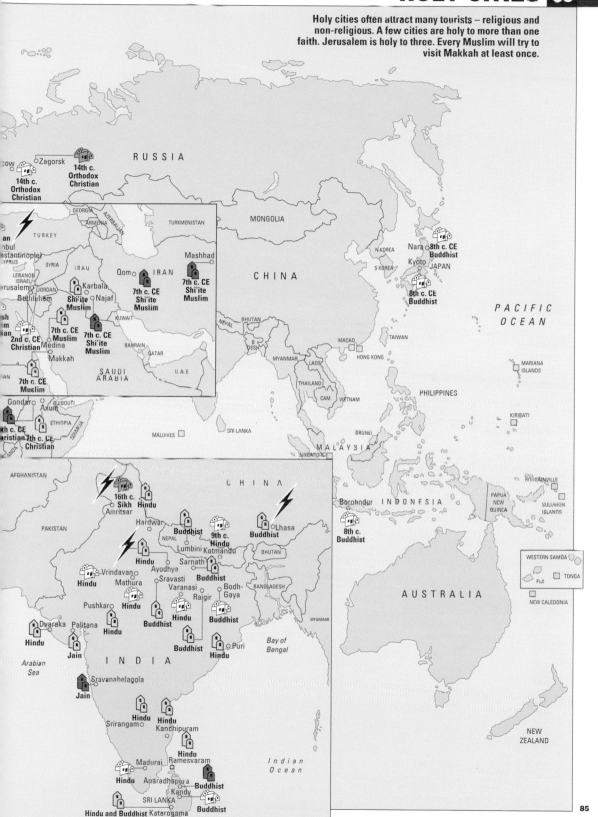

ow ☐ Zagorsk
14th c.
Orthodox
Christian
14th c.
Orthodox
Christian

RUSSIA

GEORGIA
ARMENIA   AZERBAIJAN
TURKMENISTAN

MONGOLIA

an
TURKEY
bul
nstantinople)
CYPRUS
LEBANON   SYRIA   IRAQ
ISRAEL
rusalem   JORDAN
Bethlehem   Karbala
Shi'ite   Najaf
Muslim
KUWAIT
BAHRAIN
2nd c. CE   QATAR
Christian   Medina
Makkah
SAUDI
ARABIA   U.A.E
7th c. CE
Muslim

Qom   IRAN
7th c. CE
Shi'ite
Muslim

Mashhad
7th c. CE
Shi'ite
Muslim

CHINA

N-KOREA
S-KOREA
Nara ☐ 8th c. CE
Buddhist
Kyoto   JAPAN
8th c. CE
Buddhist

PACIFIC
OCEAN

MARIANA
ISLANDS

sh
m
an   MACAO
TAIWAN
HONG KONG

PHILIPPINES

KIRIBATI

AN
Gondar   Axum
th c. CE   ETHIOPIA
ristian 7th c. CE
Christian
DJIBOUTI
SOMALIA

MALDIVES ☐   SRI LANKA

MYANMAR
LAOS
THAILAND
CAM   VIETNAM
MALAYSIA
SINGAPORE
BRUNEI

Borobudur   INDONESIA
8th c.
Buddhist

BOUGAINVILLE
PAPUA
NEW
GUINEA
SOLOMON
ISLANDS

AFGHANISTAN

16th c.
Sikh   Hindu
Amritsar
Hardwar
PAKISTAN
NEPAL
Hindu
Buddhist   9th c.
Hindu
Lumbini Katmandu   Lhasa
Buddhist
Vrindavan   Sarnath
Hindu   Ayodhya
Mathura   Sravasti   Buddhist
Pushkar☐   Varanasi
Hindu   Raigir   Bodh-
Gaya
Dvaraka   Buddhist   Buddhist
Hindu   Hindu
Hindu   Palitana
Jain

CHINA

BHUTAN
BANGLADESH
Puri
Hindu

Bay of
Bengal

AUSTRALIA

MYANMAR

Arabian
Sea

INDIA

Sravanabelagola
Jain

Hindu   Hindu
Srirangam   Kanchipuram
Hindu
Ramesvaram
Hindu
Madurai
Anaradhapura
Kandy
SRI LANKA
Hindu and Buddhist Katarogama
Buddhist
Buddhist

Indian
Ocean

NEW
ZEALAND

WESTERN SAMOA
FIJI   ☐ TONGA
☐
NEW CALEDONIA

GREENLAND
(Den)

SVALBARD &
JA N MAYEN ISLANDS

C A N A D A

ICELAND

**Iona
Christian**

**Lindisfarne
Christian**

NORWAY

SWEDEN

**Croagh Patrick
Christian**

IRELAND

UNITED
KINGDOM

DENMARK

NETH.
BEL.

GERMANY

CZ

U N I T E D   S T A T E S
O F   A M E R I C A

FRANCE
MONACO

AUS
S
ITALY

ANDORRA

HOLY SEE

PORTUGAL

SPAIN

BERMUDA

GIBRALTAR (UK)

TUNISIA

MALT

MEXICO

A T L A N T I C
O C E A N

MOROCCO

ALGERIA

LIB

WESTERN SAHARA

CUBA

BAHAMAS

DOMINICAN REPUBLIC

BELIZE

HAITI

PUERTO RICO (US)

JAMAICA

CAPE VERDE

MAURITANIA

MALI

NIGER

GUATEMALA

HONDURAS

GUADELOUPE (Fr)

SENEGAL

EL SALVADOR

MARTINIQUE (Fr)

GAMBIA

NICARAGUA

NETH. ANTILLES   GRENADA

BARBADOS

GUINEA-BISSAU

GUINEA

BURKINA
FASO

COSTA RICA

TRINIDAD & TOBAGO

SIERRA LEONE

IVORY
COAST

GHANA

BENIN

NIGERIA

PANAMA

VENEZUELA

GUYANA

LIBERIA

P A C I F I C
O C E A N

SURINAME

FRENCH GUIANA (Fr)

COLOMBIA

TOGO
EQUATORIAL GUINEA

CAMEROON

SAO TOME & PRINCIPE

GABON

ECUADOR

CONGO

PERU

B R A Z I L

AN

NA

BOLIVIA

PARAGUAY

CHILE

URUGUAY

ARGENTINA

HOLY PLACES

NATURAL SITES AS CENTRES OF
DEVOTION FOR MAJOR WORLD
RELIGIONS *1993*

islands

mountains

rivers

Sources: S. Naquin and Chûn-sang Yû, eds.
Pilgrimages and Sacred Sites in China, 1992;
H.J. Richards, *Pilgrimage to the Holy Land*,
1982; personal communications

FALKLAND ISLANDS
(UK)

**Mt. Carmel
Jewish and
Christian**

**Mt. Tabor
Jewish and
Christian**

**River Jordan
Christian**

**Dome of the Rock
Muslim and
Jewish**

Jerusalem

**Mt. Sinai
Jewish, Muslim
and Christian**

Some elements of landscape are revered not just for
their beauty, but for their association with a key
religious figure or event.

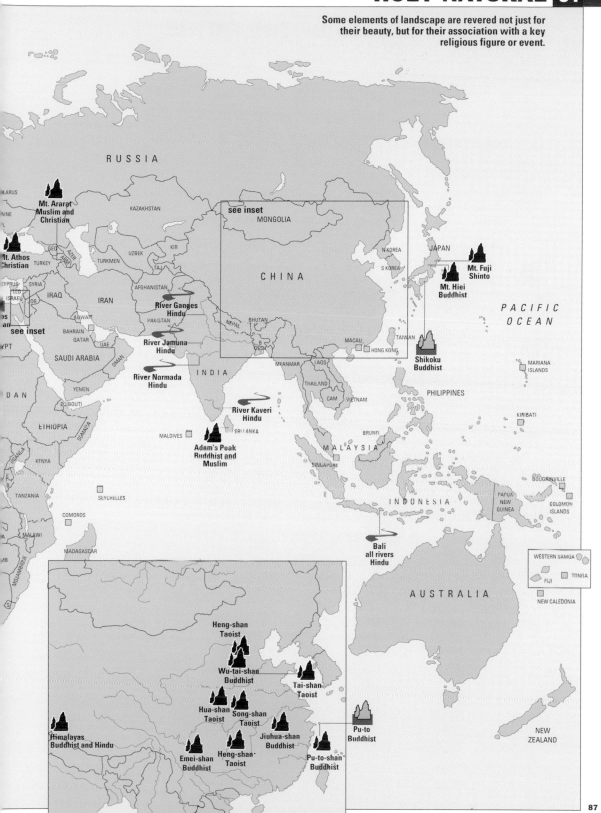

RUSSIA

KAZAKHSTAN

MONGOLIA

see inset

CHINA

Mt. Ararat
Muslim and
Christian

Mt. Athos
Christian

GEO

ARM AZER

TURKEY

TURKMEN

UZBEK

TAJ

KIR

N.KOREA

S.KOREA

JAPAN

Mt. Fuji
Shinto

Mt. Hiei
Buddhist

CYPRUS

SYRIA

LEB

ISRAEL

IRAQ

JOR

IRAN

AFGHANISTAN

River Ganges
Hindu

PAKISTAN

NEPAL

BHUTAN

see inset

BAHRAIN

QATAR

UAE

OMAN

KUWAIT

River Jamuna
Hindu

B
DESH

MACAU

TAIWAN

MYANMAR

LAOS

PACIFIC
OCEAN

PT

SAUDI ARABIA

YEMEN

River Normada
Hindu

INDIA

HONG KONG

Shikoku
Buddhist

THAILAND

CAM

VIETNAM

PHILIPPINES

MARIANA
ISLANDS

DAN

DJIBOUTI

ETHIOPIA

SOMALIA

River Kaveri
Hindu

MALDIVES

SRI LANKA

BRUNEI

M A L A Y S I A

KIRIBATI

Adam's Peak
Buddhist and
Muslim

SINGAPORE

KENYA

UGANDA

SEYCHELLES

I N D O N E S I A

PAPUA
NEW
GUINEA

BOUGAINVILLE

SOLOMON
ISLANDS

TANZANIA

COMOROS

MALAWI

MADAGASCAR

MOZAMBIQUE

MB

Bali
all rivers
Hindu

A U S T R A L I A

WESTERN SAMOA

FIJI

TONGA

NEW CALEDONIA

NEW
ZEALAND

Heng-shan
Taoist

Wu-tai-shan
Buddhist

Tai-shan
Taoist

Hua-shan
Taoist

Song-shan
Taoist

Jiuhua-shan
Buddhist

Pu-to
Buddhist

Himalayas
Buddhist and Hindu

Emei-shan
Buddhist

Heng-shan
Taoist

Pu-to-shan
Buddhist

FUNDAMENTALS OF THE FAITHS

THE NATURE OF GOD

BUDDHISM

Buddhists generally recognize the existence of 'supernatural' or god-like beings, but do not believe in an omnipotent creator God. All Buddhists recognize a transcendent truth and some conceive this in terms of a 'Buddha Nature' which infuses everything.

CHRISTIANITY

Christians believe in one God, creator of all things, considered to be three 'persons', the Trinity: God the Father, the Son (Jesus Christ) and the Holy Spirit.
These three aspects of God co-exist within one Godhead.

HINDUISM

Hindus believe in one Godhead or Divine Power, with innumerable forms. Three major forms are: Brahma, creator of each universe; Vishnu, sustainer and defender; and Shiva, destroyer and re-creator. Vishnu has ten main forms or avatars which come to the help of the universe. These include Krishna and Rama.

ISLAM

Muslims believe there is one God, Allah. (Arabic for God). Allah is indivisible, has no equals, is the creator of all and has spoken to humanity through many prophets, of whom Muhammad is the last.

JUDAISM

One God (whose name must not be pronounced), who created all things and who through his special covenant with the Jews has guided human life and destiny.

SIKHISM

One God, who is the true Guru (teacher). Unbound by time or space and beyond human definition, he makes himself known to those who are ready.

TAOISM

Taoists believe in universal forces of nature – yin and yang. Through creative tension with each other they keep the world spinning and moving. Popular Taoism has thousands of gods but Taoists do not believe in a single supreme God.

THE CREATION

BUDDHISM

 For Buddhists the Creation is cyclical, having no start and no end. It is part of the wheel of suffering to which we are attached through re-birth. Creation is seen as just part of this wheel.

CHRISTIANITY

 All that exists does so through God who began creation at a definite point in time and who will end creation. God created from nothing and all that he creates has purpose and meaning.

HINDUISM

 Creation is cyclical. From the destruction of a previous universe, Brahma arises to create a new universe; Vishnu sustains it through a cycle of birth, growth and decline; Shiva destroys the universe and the cycle begins again.

ISLAM

 God is the creator. He simply says 'Be' and all things exist. God guides his creation and has a purpose for all forms of life within creation.

JUDAISM

 God is the creator and the Book of Genesis says he created in six days and rested on the seventh. God will end creation in his own time.

SIKHISM

 God is the creator of all, so all life is good. Attachment to this world means rebirth, so that release from this world is the highest goal.

TAOISM

 Creation as an event is not of great importance. There are various stories. In essence, the twin forces of yin and yang were created from nothing rather than by any being, and from these twin forces come all life.

TIME

BUDDHISM

 Time is cyclical. Each existence continues through death and rebirth so long as the sense of self keeps us attached to this world. Individual desires are finally quenched (nirvana) but the world continues on its cyclical pattern. Some forms of Buddhism believe in a future Buddha who will come and bring release to all beings.

CHRISTIANITY

 Time is linear, though there are two very different approaches. In one, there is the suggestion that through human lives a renewed and peaceful world will be created – the Kingdom of God on earth. In the second, the world becomes so full of suffering and wrongdoing that an antichrist will appear, bringing conflict. Christ then returns and defeats the antichrist in a great battle inaugurating a reign of peace.

HINDUISM

 Time is cyclical. The world passes through various stages, from birth to growth to decline. We are currently in Kali Yuga, the age of decline. The world will eventually be destroyed, only for a new world to appear in the distant future.

ISLAM

 Time is linear. At the end of time, God will announce the Judgement Day and the world will end. All will be judged on that day.

JUDAISM

 Time is linear. The Messiah, or the Chosen One of God, will come when either the world has become a better place or when it has reached the point of greatest trouble. The Messiah will herald an era of world peace.

SIKHISM

 Time is cyclical and beliefs associated with time are similar to those of Hinduism.

TAOISM

 There are elements of both the linear and the cyclical. There is no end to the world, just a personal journey, either to better and better rebirths, or into immortality.

LIFE AFTER DEATH

BUDDHISM

At death, each life continues in some other form – human, divine or animal, depending upon the results of behaviour in the last life. The goal of Buddhism is to extinguish the flame of wanting or attachment to the sense of self so that rebirth does not occur and Nirvana is attained.

CHRISTIANITY

There is one life only. Beliefs about death vary. The soul may ascend to heaven and be judged by God; or, the soul and the body may be raised on the Day of Judgement , at the end of time, and will then be judged.

HINDUISM

Depending upon the karma – the consequences of action in this present life – at death, the soul (atman) is reborn in either a higher or lower physical form. Through devotion or correct behaviour it is possible to ascend through the orders of reincarnation, achieve liberation from the cycle of rebirth, and be reunited with the Supreme Being.

ISLAM

There is one life only. After death, the individual awaits the Day of Judgement when all will be brought back to life and judged. Paradise awaits those who have lived according to the will of God and those who have failed to do so cannot enter Paradise.

JUDAISM

There is one life only. Most religious Jews believe the individual awaits the Day of Judgement when God will raise all to life and judgement. Some, however, believe that the soul is judged immediately after death.

SIKHISM

Each individual has many reincarnations, but being born a human means the soul is nearing the end of rebirth. God judges each soul at death and may either reincarnate the soul or, if pure enough, allow it to rest with him.

TAOISM

At death, the soul is judged by up to 10 different gods of Hell, is purified by punishment then reborn again. Certain schools believe death is avoidable. By practising special meditations or eating certain things, the body is made immortal so that the person lives forever.

SACRED LITERATURE

BUDDHISM

The teachings of the Buddha are handed down in a collection of writings known as the 'Three Baskets' (*Tri-Pitaka*), comprising the discourses of the Buddha, the rules of discipline for Buddhist monks and nuns, and further knowledge – the 'great teaching basket'. Three versions survive: one in the Pali language (used by southern Buddhists) and two Mahayana versions in Chinese and in Tibetan (used by northern Buddhists). The Mahayana versions include later books not recognized as authoritative by southern Buddhists.

CHRISTIANITY

The Bible consists of the Old Testament – the books of the Hebrew Bible – plus the New Testament. The books of the New Testament were fixed c. 280 CE and are the Gospels, Acts of the Apostles, letters from writers such as Paul and James and the Book of Revelation.

HINDUISM

There are many sacred books, of which the Bhagavad Gita and the Upanishads are seen as the most important.

ISLAM

The Qur'an, dictated by the Angel Jibra'il to Muhammad in the first part of the 7th century CE. Muslims believe the Qur'an was written by God before time began.

JUDAISM

The Hebrew Bible has three parts. The Torah (Five Books of Moses), the Prophets and the Writings such as Esther and the Psalms. The Torah contains laws, doctrine and guidance on way of life, as well as accounts of the early history of the Jewish people and their relationship with God.

SIKHISM

The Guru Granth Sahib, a collection of writings and hymns by some of the 10 Gurus of Sikhism, plus material from Muslim and Hindu writers. It was compiled mid-16th century and was made the eleventh and final Guru of Sikhism at the death of the tenth Guru in 1708.

TAOISM

There are over 4000 books in the Taoist Canon, from the 4th century BCE to the 14th century CE. Each school has its own favourites and many look back to the Tao Te Ching of Lao Tzu, compiled c. 4th century BCE, as their initial source of inspiration.

PROPHETS AND FOUNDERS

BUDDHISM

The Buddha was an Indian Prince, Siddhartha Gotama, who lived in the 5th century BCE. He became known as the Enlightened One (Buddha) when he understood the cause of suffering and the way to end suffering.

CHRISTIANITY

The faith is named after Jesus Christ, who was born in Palestine c. 4 BCE and crucified c. 29 CE. Christians believe he is the Son of God, part of the Trinity and that he came to earth in human form to bring humanity back to fellowship with God.

HINDUISM

There are thousands of Hindu gurus, reflecting the huge variety of teachings. A guru, or teacher, is someone who has gained enlightenment through knowledge and practice. A Hindu wanting to follow a particular path of prayer, meditation and devotion usually has a guru.

ISLAM

Islam means to be in submission to God, who is seen as its founder. There have been numerous prophets who came to remind people of God's will, such as Abraham, Moses and Jesus. The final prophet is believed to be Muhammad who lived in the 6th–7th century CE.

JUDAISM

Through the covenant with Abraham and his descendants, God chose the Jews as his special people. This covenant was reaffirmed and consolidated with Moses, when God gave Moses the Law by which Israelites were to live.

SIKHISM

Guru Nanak (1469–1539) was the first Guru of Sikhism and was followed by nine more human Gurus. The tenth and last was Guru Gobind Singh (1675–1780), who appointed the Scriptures, the Granth Sahib, as the final Guru.

TAOISM

There have been various figures, ranging from mythical emperors to semi-historical figures such as Lao Tzu (5th century BCE) and Chang Tao Ling (2nd century CE), who founded popular Taoism.

RITES OF BIRTH AND DEATH

BUDDHISM

 Buddhists invite monks and nuns to attend such events and to read the scriptures, but the main ceremonies are generally from older traditions. In Theravada Buddhism, funerals are occasions for teaching about suffering and impermanence and for chanting *paritta* (protection) in order to gain and transfer merit for the sake of the deceased.

CHRISTIANITY

 Many Christians are baptized into the Church while they are babies, but this can be done at any time in life. At death, Christians are laid to rest in the hope of the resurrection of the dead. Cremation or burial are both acceptable.

HINDUISM

 Before birth and in the first months of life, there are many ceremonies. These include: reciting the scriptures to the baby in the womb; casting its horoscope when it is born; cutting its hair for the first time. At death, bodies are cremated and the ashes thrown on to a sacred river. The River Ganges is the most sacred river of all.

ISLAM

 At birth, the call to prayer is whispered into the baby's ear. After seven days the baby is given a name, shaved, and baby boys are circumcized. At death, the body is washed as if ready for prayer and then buried as soon as possible. Cremation is not allowed.

JUDAISM

 Baby boys are circumcized eight days after birth. The names of girls are announced in the synagogue on the first Sabbath after birth. Burial takes place within 24 hours of death and cremation is very rare. The family is in full mourning for seven days and, for eleven months, the special prayer Kadish is said every day.

SIKHISM

 At birth, the Mool mantra, the core teaching of Sikhism, is whispered into the baby's ear. The baby is named at the gurdwara, or place of worship. The Guru Granth Sahib is opened and the first letter of the first word on the page gives the first letter of the baby's name. At death, the body is cremated and the ashes thrown on to running water.

TAOISM

 Horoscopes are cast at birth. After a month a naming ceremony is held. At death, the body is buried and paper models of money, houses and cars are burnt to help the soul in the afterlife. After about 10 years the body is dug up and the bones buried again in an auspicious site.

FESTIVALS

BUDDHISM

Wesak celebrates the life of the historical Buddha (May–June). Dhammacakka celebrates the Buddha's first sermon where he taught the principles of Buddhism (July).

CHRISTIANITY

The main festivals celebrate the life of Jesus Christ: Christmas, celebrating his birth (25 December); Easter, marking his death and resurrection (March–April); Ascension Day, celebrating his return to Heaven (May). Pentecost celebrates the coming of the Holy Spirit onto the Disciples (May–June).

HINDUISM

There are many festivals, of which the main ones are: Mahashivaratri celebrating Shiva (February–March); Holi, the harvest festival in honour of love and of Krishna (March–April); Divali, celebrating the New Year and Rama and Sita, central figures of The Ramayana, a Hindu epic (October–November).

ISLAM

The Muslim calendar is lunar and moves 11 days earlier each year, compared with the Western solar calendar. The months given here are for 1993–95. Ramadan is the month of fasting (February); Eid ul Fitr marks the end of Ramadan and the giving of the Qur'an to Muhammad (March); Eid ul Adha is the time of the Hajj, the pilgrimage to Makkah and celebrates the obedience of the Prophet Ibrahim (May–June).

JUDAISM

Passover or Pesach celebrates the exodus of the Jews from Egypt (March–April); Shavuot, or Pentecost, marks the giving of the Law to Moses (May–June); Rosh Hashanah is the New Year festival, and Yom Kippur, the day of repentance (both in September–October); Hanukkah celebrates the survival of the Jews (December).

SIKHISM

Baisakhi celebrates the foundation of the Khalsa (13 April); other major festivals include the Martyrdom of Guru Arjan Dev (May–June); the birthday of Guru Nanak, the founder of Sikhism (November); the Martyrdom of Guru Tegh Bahadur (November); and the birthday of Guru Gobind Singh (December).

TAOISM

There are hundreds of local festivals. The main festivals: Chinese New Year (January–February); Ching Ming, for the veneration of the dead (4 or 5 April); the Hungry Ghosts' festival for the release of the restless dead; the Moon Festival, celebrating the harvest moon (September–October).

NOTES TO THE MAPS

1 POPULAR RELIGIONS

While the majority of the world's population (80 percent) claims some religious allegiance, what this means differs from state to state and even from faith to faith. In both Islam and Hinduism, the notion that religion is separate from life is unthinkable. In many states, Islam describes itself as a way of life rather than as a faith; and Hinduism as a term of reference to a 'faith' is something of an external creation. The name was introduced by the Persians to describe all beliefs in India – across the River Indus. Hindus themselves see what they believe as being how they live. There is no sense of one set of beliefs for everyday life and another for religious life. Judaism is also particular, since it is both a way of life and an ethnic identity – not always linked to religious belief or practice.

For many people, religious identity goes hand in hand with ethnic, social and cultural identity. Thus questions about how much a faith is practised are not really appropriate to, say, Indonesia, or large swathes of Africa, Latin America or even China. For most people, their faith is not a matter of conscious choice. They are born into a given set of values and beliefs. Unless some major trauma shakes them or they move right out of their own culture, the faith of their birth remains their faith throughout life. This pattern can be disturbed. Certain faiths and New Religious Movements are committed to conversion, and the arrival of missionaries may also change religious allegiance. This is clearly shown in the decline of traditional beliefs worldwide since 1450 (see **2. Arrivals**).

In Christianity, the notion of religion as separate from life is largely a Protestant north European/North American idea, but its impact has been immense. Because much academic study of religion has sprung from northern Europe and North America, the Protestant division into a public, secular world and a private, religious world has coloured how religion is understood. This in turn has led to a greater marginalization of religion from social life, and not just in those areas where the secular/religious division is a historic one. Modern India has tried to restrain or contain religion by using this model of a divide between the secular and religious. The secular constitution it adopted on independence was a direct legacy of rule by a colonial power, and this artificial divide may well be contributing to present tensions in India.

In those areas where religions are expanding fast – notably in the states which replaced the former USSR and in Africa – religious commitment often carries with it powerful social, political and ethnic identity. A change in religion is often also a social and political statement.

In northern Europe, Australia and New Zealand the situation is very different. While a majority claim allegiance to a faith, under 50 percent on average attend church on a regular basis (see inset, 'Empty Pews'). The USA, while to a great extent sharing what is seen as a common 'secular' culture with northern Europe, has developed a high level of church attendance amongst those professing a faith. However it would be a mistake to equate religious life with church attendance. The recent growth of interest in religious and spiritual issues in 'secular' cultures is testimony to a growing willingness to explore such areas, albeit not necessarily through conventional channels. Nevertheless, there is in these countries a continued steady growth in secularism – also often to be found in the educated urban classes outside Western Europe.

Empty pews highlight the gap between professed belief and practice, but TV and radio are another common means of worship throughout Europe. Church attendance in Norway, for example, has historically never been high due to the distances between places of worship and extremes of climate. But over 50 percent listen to the Sunday morning service on radio or TV. In Western Europe overall, however, the decline in weekly attendance at a place of worship does indicate a decline of religious observance.

Sources to the map:

Barrett, David B., *World Christian Encyclopedia*, Nairobi: Oxford University Press, 1982; Brierley, Peter, ed., *UK Christian Handbook 1992–3*, London: MARC Europe, 1992; Harris, Ian and others, eds., *Contemporary Religions*, Harlow: Longman, 1992; Harvey, Peter, *An Introduction to Buddhism*, Cambridge: Cambridge University Press, 1990; Horrie, Chris and Peter Chippindale, *What is Islam?*, London: Virgin, 1991; Shaikh, Farzana, ed., *Islam and Islamic Groups*, Harlow: Longman, 1992.

2 ARRIVALS

By 1450, Christianity appeared to be almost exclusively a white European religion, while Islam, with its heartlands in the Middle East, was primarily an Arab and Turkic religion. From the 1450s onwards, both Christianity and Islam began a new phase of expansion. Christianity, because of advances in navigation, moved out by boat to travel the world, starting with the voyages of Henry the Navigator. His Portuguese sailors crept their way round the northern coast of Africa, making the first new European landfall in West Africa in 1445. This landfall explains the early arrival of Christianity in Equatorial Guinea; and these early voyages opened the way for the major expeditions of the late 15th century.

In Islam, the fall of Constantinople in 1453 left the way clear for a sweep of the Ottoman Empire right across Eastern Europe to the gates of Vienna. Islam also experienced a revival in many traditional Muslim areas as a response to the increase in Christian missionary work which followed the explorers' ships. This in turn led to renewed Islamic mission especially in North Africa and India.

The development of Christianity was the more dramatic. By the newly-discovered trade routes across the seas, West European nations such as Spain, Portugal, England and the Netherlands, took both Christianity and colonialism around the world. The 'discovery' of the Americas was to have the greatest impact, but the spread of Christianity around the coastline of West, Southern and East Africa and into parts of Southeast Asia marked a major shift in the religious alignment of these large areas. By land, Russia was to colonize and Christianize Siberia from the 1600s onwards.

Following the capture of Constantinople in 1453, Islam spread into Europe yet more deeply. At one point in the 17th century, the Muslim Ottoman Empire controlled Greece, Bulgaria, Romania, Hungary and the area of former Yugoslavia. This proved to be a passing phase. More significant was its deeper penetration into North Africa and into Southeast Asia, consolidating and expanding its presence in both areas throughout the last four hundred years.

At that time most of the rest of the world, including the Americas, Australasia and the majority of Africa, practised local traditional religions, largely unaffected by any major world religion. Unlike Christianity or Islam, none of these cultures made universal claims for their teachings, nor did they experience the missionary drive which propelled Christianity and Islam across the world.

The expansion of Christianity and Islam rudely altered the world. Christianity, in particular, brought with it colonization and the impact of Western religion, diseases, and slavery reduced the numbers of indigenous peoples dramatically. In certain areas, indigenous faiths were literally wiped out. This, combined with major programmes for the conversion of indigenous peoples by both religions, has led to the virtual eclipse of indigenous religions in vast areas of the world. (For areas in which they have survived, see **9. Traditional Beliefs**.)

The rise of Marxism/Leninism and its associated secularism had a formidable impact on the practice of Buddhists, Christians, Jews and Muslims throughout the world. Communist states contributed more than any other cause to the persecution of faiths and loss of religious power. The collapse of Communism in the former USSR and Eastern Europe in 1991 has resulted in a remarkable revitalization. Religion is being rediscovered even where Communism is still powerful and asserting official disapproval, as in China and North Korea. Religious revival is not just an attempt to return to the past, for the faiths have all been changed by their experience. The survival of religious teachings, practices and beliefs where no outward sign is permissible (for example, Albania, 1967-91, or China during the Cultural Revolution, 1966-76) has taken many by surprise.

The dates given on the map indicate the first recorded arrival of a new faith, other than that which prevailed before 1450.

Sources to the map:
G. Barraclough, ed., *The Times Concise Atlas of World History*, London: HarperCollins, 1988; Barrett, David B., *Cosmos, Chaos and Gospel*, Birmingham, Alabama: New Hope, 1987; Barrett, David B., *World Christian Encyclopedia*, Nairobi: Oxford University Press, 1982; Shaikh, Farzana, ed., *Islam and Islamic Groups*, Harlow: Longman, 1992.

3 ROOTS AND BRANCHES

The roots of religious change and division are diverse. They do not necessarily stem from theology and may owe much to political, economic, and social issues.

When a faith moves across borders and cultures, it may have to adapt to new conditions. New forms may develop, different from or even at odds with more traditional interpretations. Buddhism, for example, spread from its original homeland in India, into China, Tibet and Japan. Many new schools of Buddhism arose that were not in conflict with earlier traditions, but made sense within the new cultures.

Political and ethnic differences may also create new schools, divisions or denominations. The success of the Protestant Reformation in 16th-century Europe owes as much to the rise of nationalism, expressed through the evolution of such 'national' churches as the Church of Sweden or the Church of England, as it does to substantial theological disagreement.

Some divisions have arisen from the desire of people to make a faith their own and from resistance to religious authority. Local expressions of an international faith may be allowed – even encouraged – as a source of vitality.

The key denominations, schools and groups within the major faiths are given below. There are myriad smaller ones including, for example, as many as 20,000 Christian denominations.

Buddhism. There are two major divisions, the Southern school, known as Theravada, and the Northern school, Mahayana. Theravada or 'Teaching of the Elders' is considered to be the oldest school and its holy books, the Pali Canon, the ones closest to the words of the historical Buddha. The Pali Canon has shaped Buddhism in Sri Lanka, Myanmar, Thailand and much of South-east Asia. Mahayana or 'Great Vehicle' arose around 2000 years ago and its teachings have shaped Buddhism throughout China, Korea, Japan, Tibet and Mongolia.

Christianity. There are three major divisions. The Roman Catholic Church and Orthodox Church, originally the eastern and western wings of the same Church, finally split into two sections in 1054. Differences over interpretation of authority and theology brought out tensions between the newer, Eastern Roman empire based on Constantinople and the older Western Roman empire based on Rome. The 16th-century Protestant revolution reacted against Roman Catholicism and created new denominations. Some, such as Lutherans and Anglicans, essentially continued the old style of Church with bishops and other Catholic practices, but made kings head of the Church, rather than the Pope. Over time, other Protestant denominations developed which rejected bishops and the Catholic theology of the state churches. Presbyterians, Congregationalists or Quakers all sought to develop models of leadership and theology which they believed were those practised by the early Church.

Hinduism. Hinduism is not really a single faith so it is not appropriate to suggest divisions. Hindus often refer to their faith as Sanatana Dharma or Eternal Truth, one of its ancient names. There continue to be hundreds of different ways that this is expressed, the two main forms being Vaishnavite (special devotion to Vishnu) and Shaivite (special devotion to Shiva).

Islam. In the mid-7th century CE, Islam divided, over the source of religious authority within the faith, into two major divisions, Sunni and Shi'a. The word Sunni derives from the Arabic 'code of behaviour', the body of traditional law that derives from the teachings and acts of the Prophet Muhammad. Sunni Muslims hold that the first three caliphs were all Muhammad's true successors and Sunnis form the majority of Muslims. They follow one of four main schools of law, Hanafi, Hanbali, Maliki or Shafi, all founded by Muslim jurists in the 8th and early 9th centuries.

The Shi'a believe that Ali was Muhammad's first true successor and the term Shi'a originally referred to the partisans (shi'a) of Ali. There are a number of major sub-groups, the largest being the Ithna'shaariyya (the Twelvers), so-called because they believe that the

twelfth imam of the line of Ali was not murdered and did not die when he disappeared at 4 years old. They believe he will reappear as the al-Mahdi – the chosen one – who will herald the end of the world. The Zayids are a further sub-group. They were founded by the 5th imam after Ali and are now found primarily in the Yemen.

The Ibadiyah was the first group to split away from the main body of Islam, while claiming to preserve the true teachings of Islam. Based on a group around Khadijah, the Prophet Muhammad's wife and first convert to Islam, they are very strict in their observance and have little contact with other Muslim groups.

Judaism. Since the map shows only the divisions of majority religions, Jewish groups do not appear. Orthodox Jews, who are in the majority, assert the supreme authority of the Torah and believe that Jewish laws are not open to revision. Moves away from traditional or 'orthodox observance' have given rise to Reform, Liberal, Conservative, Reconstructionist and other forms of Judaism.

Sikhism. There is no major doctrinal division within Sikhism, but Sikhs are increasingly divided over whether or not there should be an independent Sikh political state – Khalistan – carved out of India and possibly part of Pakistan.

Taoism. The Taoism best known in the West is often called 'philosophical' Taoism after the great mystic writers Lao Tzu, Chuang Tzu and Lieh Tzu of the 5th to 3rd centuries BCE. However most Taoism as actually practised comes from what is called 'religious' Taoism founded by Chang Tao Ling in the 2nd century CE. Many different schools emerged over the next thousand years though only a few survive in any significant form today. Much of popular Chinese indigenous religion is Taoist-influenced, with a strong overtone of Chinese popular Buddhism.

In countries where there are different faiths or divisions, we have given details only for those forming the majority. The USA, for example, appears as majority Protestant, but within the Protestant majority, the Southern Baptists are the largest Protestant denomination, hence the symbol for Baptists.

Sources to the map:
Barrett, David B., *World Christian Encyclopedia*, Nairobi: Oxford University Press, 1982; Harvey, Peter, *An Introduction to Buddhism*, Cambridge: Cambridge University Press, 1990; Horrie, Chris and Peter Chippindale, *What is Islam?*, London: Virgin, 1991; Shaikh, Farzana, ed , *Islam and Islamic Groups*, Harlow: Longman, 1992.

Acknowledgements:
Rupert Gethin.

4   CHRISTIANITY AND ISLAM

In the early 1990s, the two largest religions in the world are Christianity, with 1870 million adherents, and Islam, with 1014 million. Numerically, these are also the two fastest-growing faiths.

Christianity is growing across the world, especially in South Korea, Russia and sub-Saharan Africa. Islam is also growing worldwide, especially in the Muslim states of the former USSR. Both faiths are expanding largely through population increase: Christianity, in Europe (although in much of Western Europe populations are slowing down for other reasons), Russia, the Americas, Australasia and now in sub-Saharan Africa; Islam, in the Middle East, Central Asia, North Africa and Indonesia/Malaysia.

Both Christianity and Islam have explicit missionary teachings within their sacred books and within the tradition of the faith. While other faiths have an element of mission – usually seen as being carried out through personal contact and friendship – organizations within Christianity and Islam place a structural and financial emphasis upon taking their message to other peoples, as well as to non-practising members of their own faith (for the Christian missionary movement, see **14. The Mission**).

The two faiths are in most direct competition where sizeable populations still adhere to traditional beliefs. In Nigeria, Kenya or Tanzania, for example, the expansion of either Christianity or Islam is usually at the expense of local traditional religions, rather than each other.

While there are many small Christian communities in Muslim majority countries, often pre-dating Islam, their numbers are remaining static or decreasing through migration (as in Syria, Egypt or the Lebanon). However, there are large numbers of Filipinos, Korean and Christians from other countries, living and working across Muslim heartlands. There are also growing, active Muslim minorities in Western Europe. These communities, which began through links created by Western colonialism, have continued to expand through family connections or migrant labour from Muslim countries, and by acquiring converts from the host community.

Both faiths have found some cultures resistant. India and China, despite centuries of effort, have proved difficult for Christians to penetrate. In India, Christians are a tiny minority. In China, until very recently, never more than 1 percent of Chinese would call themselves Christian. For Islam, India has been a place of conquest and then retreat. In China, Islam has never reached beyond the Turkomanic and Mongolian tribes which it converted in the early centuries of Islam.

Sources to the map:
Barrett, David B., *World Christian Encyclopedia*, Nairobi: Oxford University Press, 1982; Barrett, David B., and Todd M. Johnson, eds., *Our Globe and How to Reach It*, Birmingham, Alabama: New Hope, 1990; Brierley, Peter, ed., *UK Christian Handbook 1992–3*, London: MARC Europe, 1992; Harris, Ian and others, eds., *Contemporary Religions*, Harlow: Longman, 1992; Horrie, Chris and Peter Chippindale, *What is Islam?*, London: Virgin, 1991; Shaikh, Farzana, ed. *Islam and Islamic Groups*, Harlow: Longman, 1992; *Mainstream*, Journal of Christian Action for East-West Reconciliation, London, 1982.

Acknowledgements:
Mawil Izzi Dien.

5 HINDUISM

Hinduism is an all-embracing term to describe a vast array of beliefs, deities and traditions. Most Indians would not define themselves as Hindus. Indeed it could almost be said that religion in India is a complex web of indigenous beliefs. However there are certain key features of religious life which show a common root and understanding.

Most Hindus would accept a cyclical view of time, as being without origin and without destination. All is reincarnated, even the very gods themselves, and all is subject to change. Also most Hindus believe that the divine permeates everything, everything is divine and therefore mirrors or reflects the image of the divine. This captures the many ways of expressing belief in Sanatana Dharma – the Eternal Truth, and foundation of all life and reality. Hindus often refer to Vedic culture as being their own. This derives from the Vedas, the oldest Indian sacred books, and from which many of the essential tenets of Indian religious and social life derive.

There have been two significant phases of Hindu migration. From c.70 to 500 CE Hinduism was introduced to much of Southeast Asia and Indonesia along trade routes. Within Indonesia, it is the majority religion of Bali and is undergoing a revival on Java. The second phase began when Indians migrated to other parts of the British Empire, for example the Caribbean and Fiji, as indented labourers and for trade. Many of these communities have continued to grow through migration because of their strong links with specific areas of India. Most Hindu communities abroad co-exist peacefully, but occasionally, tension surfaces. In Uganda in 1972, 70,000 Asians were expelled by dictator Idi Amin. Many migrated to the UK.

The spread of Hindu ideas has been considerable throughout Europe, North America and Australasia. Hindu gurus have travelled west in response to the coming of Christian missionaries to India; and Westerners have been profoundly affected by visiting India and by translations of Hindu classics such as the Bhagavad Gita or the Upanishads. Hindu belief, imagery and philosophy offers a very different form of religious understanding from that practised in the West. It has created a wave of groups inspired by Hindu philosophy and practice – ranging from overtly religious movements such as the Ramakrishna Vedanta Mission to yoga and Hindu meditation. This has led to a revival of devotional Hinduism amongst many Hindus as well as attracting converts from other faiths and cultures.

The Jains are a distinct religious group whose founder Mahavira, broke away from the prevailing norms of Hinduism in the 5th century BCE. The Jains practise *ahimsa*, non-violence, and their religious orders of monks and nuns live in such a way as to minimalize harm to any living being. The most devout wear a gauze mask over their mouths to prevent them accidentally swallowing any insect, and they brush the path before them to remove ants and other insects. They believe that Mahavira was the last in a line of 24 *tirthankaras* (bridge-builders between this world and the spiritual world). The Jains have been a clearly identifiable community for over 2500 years.

Sources to the map:
Barrett, David B., *World Christian Encyclopedia* , Nairobi: Oxford University Press, 1982; Hinnells, J.R. ed., *A Handbook of Living Religions*, Harmondsworth: Penguin, 1984; Jackson, Robert, and Dermot Killingley, *Approaches to Hinduism*, London: John Murray, 1988; Williams, Raymond Brady, *Religion of Immigrants from India and Pakistan: New Threads in the American Tapestry*, Cambridge: Cambridge University Press, 1988.

Acknowledgements:
Ranchor Prime; Megan Rees.

6 BUDDHISM

Buddhism originated in north India, founded by Siddhartha Gotama, known as the Buddha – Enlightened One – in the 5th century BCE. For over a thousand years it flourished there, sending out teachers south and west to Sri Lanka, Myanmar, Thailand, Cambodia and Vietnam and north to Tibet, China and Japan. It then declined in India itself under the impact of Islam in the 10th to 12th centuries CE. Teaching that life is suffering and that attachment to suffering causes rebirth, Buddhism seeks to free the individual from the effects of suffering and ultimately from the effects of constant rebirth.

In the last 75 years, Buddhism has been subjected to more sustained persecution than at any previous time. Mongolia, a majority Buddhist country, became the second Communist state in the world in 1921. Communism took over China and then parts of Southeast Asia from the end of the Second World War until the 1970s. Thousands of monasteries were destroyed – Tibet lost virually all its monasteries - and most monks and nuns were forced out. In 1930 there were an estimated 738,200 monks and nuns in China; by 1986, there were only 28,000. In the early 1990s, Communism has lost some of its power and authority but still rules in China and elsewhere. However even where severe persecution persists, Buddhism is reviving.

Buddhism remains the religion of the majority in Thailand, Myanmar and Sri Lanka. It has recently become the majority religion again in Mongolia, as a result of new political freedoms. There are small pockets of Buddhists in Russia, in the republics of Buryat, Tuva and Kalmyk. They claim their Buddhist heritage from Mongolia. By the early 1990s Buddhism had gained strength in Indonesia, South Korea, Nepal, India, and China (though not in Tibet).

Buddhism is the state religion of Thailand and of Bhutan, a Himalayan kingdom which only recently opened itself to the outside world. There is likely to be a small Buddhist temple in most villages and in the rainy season the numbers of monks in Southeast Asian countries can double due to the number of young men taking temporary ordination. The Myanmar government is not anti-Buddhist, although increasing political and economic discontent has led to anti-government demonstrations and there is friction between monastic communities and the government.

In Japan, both Buddhism and Shintoism – the indigenous religion of Japan - are followed by the majority of people. Different temples are attended for different rites. Membership of Buddhist sects runs to 111 million. Due to traditional family affiliation many people claim membership of two or more sects, whether or not they are practising and it is impossible to gauge the actual number of practising Buddhists.

In India, the number of Buddhists has increased due to conversions, led originally by Dr B.R. Ambedkar, from the 'untouchable' castes (known as 'scheduled castes' since 1935). There has also been an influx of Buddhists fleeing from Chinese state oppression in Tibet. The spiritual leader of the Tibetans, the Dalai Lama, lives in exile in Dharamsala. While Buddhism is not under threat in most Indian states, Buddhists in Ladakh face mounting problems. Ties with Tibet have been cut off and the Muslim population is rapidly increasing. Buddhists in Bangladesh are also in difficulty, due to pressure from settlement by majority Muslim Bengalis and loss of their lands for hydro-electric schemes.

Over the last hundred years or so, Buddhism has spread throughout Europe, North America and Australia. Originally known only through translations of sacred texts and the commentaries of scholars and philosophers, since the 1960s Buddhist influence has increased as a result of great numbers of young people travelling to Buddhist countries. There is an increasing number of Buddhist centres and monasteries outside Asia, but it is virtually impossible to estimate the numbers of Westerners who practise Buddhism. Relatively few have joined organized religious orders. Many people find some aspect of Buddhist teaching, practice or belief helpful in their religious development, though they may not describe themselves as Buddhist.

Sources to the map:
Harris, Ian and others, eds., *Contemporary Religions*, Harlow: Longman, 1992; Harvey, Peter, *An Introduction to Buddhism*, Cambridge: Cambridge University Press, 1990; *International Buddhist Directory*, London: Wisdom Publicatons, 1985; Snelling, John, *The Buddhist Handbook*, London: Rider, 1987.

Acknowledgements:
Rupert Gethin; Mike Gilmore; Peter Harvey.

7 THE JEWISH DIASPORA

While numerically Jews have remained a small faith, the impact of their teachings, and in particular of the Hebrew Bible, on the world has been of greater significance than any other religious book. Both Christianity and Islam sprang from this Jewish understanding and scripture.

Most Jews today are to be found in either the USA or Israel. The state of Israel was created in 1948 – their first homeland for Jews since 70 CE when the Romans crushed a rebellion against their rule in Israel. For centuries before this, Jews had been living in scattered communities throughout the Middle East. After they were crushed by the Romans, Jews spread throughout the Roman Empire. Despite terrible persecutions and restrictions, Jews established significant communities in Spain and North Africa, Russia, Persia (modern Iran) and even India and China.

People of Jewish origin have varying degrees of personal commitment to Judaism or Israel. In fact, the numbers cited of Jews worldwide tend to vary because 'being a Jew' can have religious, ethnic or cultural meaning. In religious terms, a Jew is someone whose mother was Jewish and who lives by the Law of Moses and of the Torah – the Five Books of Moses or the first five books of the Bible. While many Jews with a Jewish mother would describe themselves as Jewish, they may well not be adherents of the faith.

The figures used in our cartogram reflect the 'core' Jewish population, namely those who clearly identify themselves as being religious Jews. This includes converts as well as those who have informally joined Jewish groups. It does not include those of Jewish descent who have no religion or follow another religion, those who were born Jewish but disclaim being Jewish, or non-Jewish members of Jewish households.

Over the last 200 years the location and size of the world's Jewish population has been radically altered: by mass migration from Europe and Russia in the late 19th to mid-20th century, mainly to the USA; by the tragedy of the Nazi Holocaust, 1939–45 (see **26. Never Again?**), which destroyed the Jewish cultures of Germany and Eastern Europe; and finally, by the creation of the state of Israel in 1948. The inset cartograms show that whereas in 1800 the vast majority of Jews lived in Europe and Russia, by the end of the 20th century the majority live in the USA or Israel.

Israel offers automatic right of entry and citizenship to any Jew from anywhere in the world. In the early 1990s, the collapse of Communism in Eastern Europe and the former USSR is allowing tens of thousands of Jews to journey to Israel (see inset map, 'The Olim') and is straining the resources of the small state.

While the Jewish population of Israel is increasing through births and immigration, elsewhere in the world the numbers are static or dropping, due to migration, marrying out and general assimilation. Thus the Jewish core population of the UK in 1977 was 336,000. By 1992, this had fallen to 301,000.

Sources to the map:
Singer, David, ed., *American Jewish Year Book*, Philadelphia, Pennsylvania: The Jewish Publication Society, 1992.

Acknowledgements:
Yitzrak Rabichiya; Marlena Schmool; Community Research Unit, Board of Deputies of British Jews; The Jewish Agency, Jerusalem.

8 SIKHISM

Sikhism arose from the teachings of Guru Nanak (1469–1539), who tried to fuse the best in Islamic and Hindu teachings and practice, combined with an intense personal revelation of the nature of God. As a result of religious persecution, the Sikhs established their own community and gained a degree of independence within Muslim-ruled India. Eventually Sikhs began to spread beyond India, especially to countries formerly part of the British Empire.

Worldwide, the number and size of Sikh communities is gradually increasing. To give a sense of the spread and relative strength of Sikhism around the world, we illustrate the number of gurdwaras. The gurdwara – or temple – is the focus of Sikh religious and community life. A community can range from a few families to a few hundred families. The presence of a gurdwara indicates a Sikh community large enough to support both it and its associated institutions.

Within India, Sikhs are migrating to the Punjab in increasing numbers. This is in response to rising levels of disturbance and tension between Sikhs and the Indian government. In turn, these are partly due to a growth of Hindu nationalism and to Sikh aspirations for their own separate state of Khalistan (Land of the Pure). In 1984, to crush the growing Sikh independence movement, Indian government troops stormed the holiest shrine of Sikhism, the Golden Temple of Amritsar.

In the early 1990s, the situation is calmer, but Sikh insurrectionists and Indian troops still clash regularly, and the political debate has riven the Sikh community. While militant Sikhs are working towards the creation of an independent state, others wish only for greater Sikh autonomy within India. Sikhs see themselves as the only major world religion without a state of their own – and many cite the creation of Israel as their model.

Sources to the map:
Cole, W. Owen, and Piara Singh Sambhi, *The Sikhs: Their Beliefs and Practices*, London: Routledge and Kegan Paul, 1978.

Acknowledgements:
W. Owen Cole.

9 TRADITIONAL BELIEFS

The terms 'traditional' and 'tribal' beliefs are here used to distinguish those cultures and belief systems which are not part of a major world religion. While they may often share certain key features – such as reverence for nature and worship or veneration of ancestors – they are not linked by adherence to any central tenets of faith. Frequently they have been part of the same geographical setting for many thousands of years and have used this setting to develop myth and ritual. It is estimated, for example, that Australian aborigine culture has existed in Australia for up to 40,000 years.

However, a few cultures have travelled. Many traditional beliefs are shaped by what is loosely called Shamanism. This is the belief that there are two worlds – a spiritual, real world, and the world of material existence. A Shaman possesses an ability to communicate with the spiritual world through trances. Shamanism is thought to have originated over 8000 years ago in Siberia and to have migrated with the movement of peoples over the landbridge linking Siberia and Alaska. Elements of Shamanism are to be found throughout the Americas.

In many parts of the world, traditional beliefs and cultures survive only in inaccessible or difficult terrain – the last refuge of peoples who formerly inhabited more accessible land but who have been pushed back by more aggressive settlers. In the Amazon basin this process is still going on (see below). In China, many of the 64 recognized minority peoples live in mountainous areas where they were driven by the spread of the Han Chinese over the last 3000 years.

Though traditional beliefs form the majority faith in few states, their influence is still widespread. In China, popular religion is observed in most villages and towns. This is a mixture of traditional beliefs focusing on ancestors, and on the intermingling of the spirit world and the physical world, overlaid with a veneer of Buddhism and Taoism. In Japan, Shintoism, unlike many traditional beliefs, has a written, rather than oral, sacred literature. **103**

Shintoism is a separate faith from Japanese Buddhism, but the two co-exist and many people follow both religions. Shintoism, like most local traditional beliefs, has neither sought nor gained a following outside its own people.

It has been the spread of Christianity and Islam that has affected traditional beliefs most dramatically over the last 500 years, fundamentally affecting the religious practice of indigenous peoples from Siberia to Africa, from the Amazon to the Australian outback. In some places, whole belief systems and formerly numerous indigenous peoples have completely disappeared.

In some areas, people have continued to practise tribal traditions as well as Christianity or Islam, which have either been changed by traditional beliefs or learned to accommodate them. The Catholic Spiritists of Brazil, for example, while clearly Roman Catholics, have incorporated specific characteristics of cults of African origin.

In some African states where Christianity or Islam has become the majority religion, traditional beliefs have mingled with them to the point of producing quite idiosyncratic expressions of faith, usually confined to a single area. The growth of 'indigenous churches' highlights the fusion of certain core Christian ideas with key elements of traditional belief. The Church of the Initiates in Gabon, for example, combines ancestor worship with specific Christian teachings and symbolism. A few churches have become missionary in their own right (see **10. New Religious Movements**).

There has recently been an increased interest in traditional beliefs amongst some people in the West. This may sometimes be a romantic quest for a physical Garden of Eden or for the Noble Savage, but such interest is bringing the insights of traditional peoples into a wider circle of religious awareness.

There has also been a revival in traditional beliefs among indigenous peoples of Australia, Canada and the USA – not always welcomed by the state. In Australia, aboriginal peoples have campaigned vigorously for the protection and return of land sacred to them, such as Ayers Rock – known as 'Uluru'. While the governments of individual Australian states have agreed to some demands, others are a continuing source of conflict. In the USA and Canada, pride in traditional beliefs and culture has led to a revival of interest, not just amongst Native Americans, but in the wider community.

Traditional beliefs and ways of life are still under threat – in some cases, at greater risk than ever before. The native peoples of the Amazon are under severe threats from logging, mining, flooding and the encroachment of ranching and urban centres. In the Sudan, pressure from northern Muslims on traditional peoples such as the Dinka has led to rebellion and warfare, endangering survival of the Dinkas' traditional way of life. Worldwide, there appears little hope that the traditions, beliefs and close links with the land of indigenous communities will remain intact.

Sources to the map:
Barrett, David B., *World Christian Encyclopedia,* Nairobi: Oxford University Press, 1982; *Sacred Spaces,* Winnipeg, Canada: Canadian Coalition for Ecology, Ethics and Religion.

Acknowledgements:
Ben Burt, Museum of Mankind, London; Ranchor Prime; Franca Tranza; Minority Rights Group, London; Survival International, London.

10 NEW RELIGIOUS MOVEMENTS

The New Religious Movements illustrated on the map have come into being since the early 19th century, but the most notable growth has been a 20th-century phenomenon. While many movements may be local only – as with the New Religions of Indonesia or the indigenous churches of Nigeria – some have moved across the world and gained a visible presence far from their place of origin. They are in fact new missionary movements, and their spread into other parts of the world is causing some alarm in areas traditionally adhering to Christianity or Islam.

Every major religion has at some time been a new religious movement, splitting away from older traditions: as Buddhism did from Hinduism, Christianity from Judaism, Sikhism from Hinduism and Islam. What marks out today's major faiths from myriad other faiths over the centuries, is their ability to survive, adapt and flourish, by speaking to the human condition.

The increase in communications this century has widely disseminated religious ideas, beliefs and teachings, throughout the world, many previously unheard of. There are over a hundred translations of the Taoist classic Tao Te Ching, enabling it to be used as a basis for a whole range of religious thought and belief, often different from its traditional use in China. The Christian Bible now appears in over 2000 languages, leading to a host of varied interpretations, often diverging from the understanding of mainstream denominations.

In some areas, traditional religious culture has been undermined by secularism and by a collapse of belief in authority. A faith may have become stuck in a particular historical model which takes no account of changing social needs or awareness; or it may be failing to re-express itself in a way which speaks to people today. In some states, institutional religion is trying to reestablish itself in the chaos reigning after decades of repression under Communism. The old church/state relationship cannot and should not be recreated. Majority religions are having to work out their new status, while the people are exposed to differing religious claims. Russia, in particular, is witnessing a wide array of new religious groups at work within its borders, not all of them genuine.

Most New Religious Movements have their roots in a major world religion. The only other movements on our map, arise from the growth of psychology and psychoanalytical methods, sometimes fusing with insights and beliefs from the frontiers of science or even from science fiction itself. Erhard Seminar Training (EST) is an example of what are termed 'self-religions' – which seek to enhance human potential through various techniques derived from psychoanalysis. The Scientologists are one of the best known of these groups. They believe that the individual is trapped by 'engrams' – negative experiences in childhood or even in the womb, which cripple and hold people back from full development. Using a system called 'Dianetics' founded by the former science fiction writer L. Ron Hubbard, they claim to be able to free the individual from these engrams and thus ensure a more fulfilled person.

New expressions of an existing faith may develop when it is transferred to a totally different culture. Buddhism, for example, was transformed as it travelled through China, producing new forms such as Chan (known as Zen in Japan) which have become part of the range of mainstream Buddhism. The opposite can happen. Ideas from another faith may be taken back home and developed within a different culture. The older religions have often disowned the activities of people who claim to be followers. The Unification Church of South Korea, for example, claims to be Christian and much of its language and symbolism comes from Christianity. Indeed, its full title is 'The Holy Spirit Association for the Unification of World Christianity'. But its leader, the Rev. Moon, believes he is the new messiah come to complete what Christ failed to achieve - the founding of a Perfect Family. Such dramatic divergence from mainstream Christian thinking means that Christianity rejects the Unification Church.

New Religious Movements often flourish in already pluralist and often volatile societies, though they rarely travel abroad. In Indonesia, over 60 million people follow indigenous New Religious Movements which are an officially recognized category of religion. In Vietnam, the Cao Dai faith and the Hoa Hao have over five million members between them.

Some New Religious Movements achieve a high public profile. They may set out to do so, like the Sanyasins of Osho (followers of Shree Rajneesh), who wear distinctive orange robes. More seriously, New Religious Movements may be accused of corruption or of abusing people through 'brainwashing' or totalitarianism. But most of them are neither sinisterly manipulative nor destructive. More often than not, they are targeted by parents or families who feel they have lost control of or contact with their children. Many more young people break off contact with their parents for reasons nothing to do with religion.

A few New Religious Movements may now be considered new religions per se. The Baha'is do not consider themselves to be a sub-group of Islam, but a new religion. They arose from Persian Islam (modern Iran) in the mid-19th century and by the end of the century had spread well beyond the Islamic world, often being embraced by those who wanted a faith similar to but not connected with Christianity. By contrast, the Ahmadiyas do consider themselves to be true Muslims, though they were rejected forcefully by mainstream Islam.

Most New Religious Movements are not the cranks and crazies of the Western popular press. They are usually serious, legitimate and highly-organized expressions of religious belief, or reworkings of older religious traditions. Many do not see themselves as having diverged from the main tradition, and often see themselves as more faithful to the original founder than the dominant expression of that faith.

Sources to the map:
Barrett, David B., *World Christian Encyclopedia*, Nairobi: Oxford University Press, 1982; Brockway, A.R., and J.P. Arjashkar, eds., *New Religious Movements and the Churches*, Geneva: WCC Publications, 1987.

Acknowledgements:
Eileen Barker; Charlotte Hardman; Ranchor Prime; The Baha'i International Community, Haifa; INFORM, London School of Economics.

11 UNITED DIVERSITY

The USA has developed prolific religious traditions and is sometimes described as offering a supermarket of religions. There are more expressions of 'Eastern' religions and New Religious Movements in the USA than anywhere else in the world – the highest concentration being probably in California. However, the vast majority of the US population professes allegiance to Christianity. With over 2500 different Christian denominations, the USA has the most diverse Christian scene in the world, though many of these denominations have one or two congregations.

Though the Protestant churches combined account for over half the US population, the largest Christian denomination is the Roman Catholics, at 30 percent. Of Protestants, the largest denomination is the Southern Baptist Convention with 14.9 million baptized members. The term 'Southern Baptist' arose when US Baptists split from the main church in 1845. Any slave owner was banned from being appointed a missionary and the Southern Baptists held a convention to oppose this ruling. In the 20th century, opposition to black civil rights has also been high in churches affiliated to the Convention, still known for their more conservative stance – even though they may have liberal members, such as President Clinton. The Southern Baptists are now found throughout the USA and overseas, where they have more missionaries than any other US church.

While the majority of Christians belong to the main denominations, their membership is declining. Roman Catholics, Southern Baptists and the Assemblies of God are holding on to their members or are increasing slowly; but Methodists, Presbyterians, Episcopalians, Disciples of Christ, United Church of Christ, Evangelical Lutherans and the Lutheran Missouri Synod, have all been declining markedly for decades. The number of Christians who attend church is much higher in the USA than other Western countries, but the dramatic growth is in those attending smaller, more local or fundamentalist/evangelical churches. Some 80,000 independent charismatic congregations have sprung up across the USA since 1980.

The TV evangelists have achieved a high profile – more for their off-station activities, such as mismanagement of finance and sexual behaviour, than for their programmes. Viewing numbers have declined in recent years and the effect of these tv stations on the religious life of the USA is small compared with their visibility.

Sources to the map:
Barrett, David B., *World Christian Encyclopedia*, Nairobi: Oxford University Press, 1982; Draper, Edythe, ed., *The Almanac of the Christian World, 1993–4*, Wheaton, Illinois: Tyndale House, 1992.

Acknowledgement:
John N. Vaughan.

12 FAITH IN THE FEMININE

The issue of patriarchy and matriarchy in world religions is a source of much heated debate within the religions themselves. All the world religions are in essence culturally patriarchal, though not necessarily so in their structural understanding of God or divine power. The founders of world religions were exclusively male (see **32. Foundations**) and their leaders are still usually male (see **29. Equal Rites**). But female figures, though not always as powerful as male figures, still have a strong presence within Christianity, Buddhism and Hinduism, if not within Islam or Judaism.

The argument rages as to whether this patriarchal dominance of religion is inherent to religion (as argued by Mary Daly and Daphne Hampson), or whether there has been a hijacking of the religious world by men (as argued by US theologian Elisabeth Schussler Fiorenza and archaeologist Marija Gimbutas). Some emphasize that there was once a pre-dominance of matriarchal religions before the rise of the major religions over the last three thousand years. Others (such as feminist Riane Eisler) point out that many world religions originally showed much greater equality between men and women, and argue that this is reflected in earlier deities and practices. This important debate, on whether the nature of differences between the sexes in authority and power is a reflection of divine planning or a construct of humanity at certain stages of evolution, has gone on since the end of the 19th century, but only seriously sustained over the last thirty years.

Feminine deities and religious figures are clearly symbolic. Is the Virgin Mary, the earth-ly mother of Jesus, whom Christians believe to have been himself divine, the archetype of the dutiful mother the Mother of God, or does she take on a divine status of her own in pop-ular religious culture? The Roman Catholic Church encourages devotion to the Virgin Mary and sightings worldwide are scrutinized by the Vatican, to minimize the influence of false claims, or claims not consistent with Roman Catholic understanding of the Virgin. Within recent years, there have been thousands of reported sightings, though few have been authenticated or proved to be of lasting significance. The Virgin often appears in places of great social and political tension.

The Chinese Buddhist deity, Kuan Yin, is the goddess of compassion and a fervent intercessor for those suffering on earth. In Hinduism, Kali may be fearfully displayed as the goddess of destruction, the consort of Shiva. She is revered as both the giver and destroy-er of life. The Tibetan deity Tara is represented in 21 different forms and in her white or green forms she symbolizes compassion, the easing of human suffering and guidance to wisdom and salvation. It is largely in this role that she is popular in the Tibet and Himalayan region. In her more menacing red, yellow or blue forms she is fearful and awe-inspiring.

Such female figures undoubtedly have a powerful impact. For some critics, these images of the mother, of the compassionate or even of the fearful, are male creations rep-resenting male wishes or fears about women. For others, the notion of the feminine divine has subversive elements and represents an awareness of either an older set of beliefs about the goddess, or a subcurrent running through history which has always seen the divine as both male and female. For yet a third group, the debate about the maleness or femaleness of God is misplaced – any such description of God is inadequate since God is experienced through faith.

Sources to the map:
Baring, A., and J. Cashford, *The Myth of the Goddess*, London: Viking Arcana, 1991; Carroll, Michael P., *The Cult of the Virgin Mary*, Princeton, New Jersey: Princeton University Press, 1992; Foy, Felician A. (O.F.M.), ed., *The Catholic Almanac 1993*, Huntington, Indiana: Our Sunday Visitor, 1992; Naquin, B.S., and Chun-sang Yu, eds., *Pilgrimages and Sacred Sites in China*, Berkeley, California: University of California Press, 1992; Snelling, John, *The Buddhist Handbook*, London: Rider, 1987.

Acknowledgements:
Caroline Davis; Celia Deane-Drummond; Sandra Palmer.

13 DOUBTS AND CERTAINTIES

The issue of religion can be very difficult for some people. Some are uncertain that they can believe anything specific about God or the divine and thus classify themselves as agnos-tics. Others define themselves as atheists, and reject all belief in God or the divine. It is not socially acceptable everywhere to profess to being an agnostic or atheist. In a handful of states, such as Iran, it is even dangerous.

In many European states, belonging to a religion no longer carries with it the notion of full adherence to a set of teachings and there exists a form of agnostic Christianity. Many people, and not just in Europe, would wish to retain moral and ethical insights and codes of faith but abandon overt religious practices. They see themselves as personally agnostic but accept the need for society to adhere to a shared moral code. When adults in the UK have been questioned about religious education, over 50 percent regarded it as important for imparting a moral code, but not so important for imparting religious faith or truths.

Those who identify themselves as atheists often do so in order to make a stance, not just against the beliefs of any given religion, but against the whole apparatus of organized religion. They may take a position that religion is not rational or subject to reasoned study and analysis, and this may be fused with personal experience of the failings of religion. Some atheists regard religious faith as being a primitive state of mind, one which hinders the fullest development of humanity. Atheism can itself become a belief system, replacing God as the centre or purpose of life with humanity or the wellbeing of the planet. Atheists have been instrumental in founding many international humanitarian agencies such as the United Nations or the International Union for Conservation of Nature and Natural Resources.

The activities of official atheist states, former or otherwise, has caused problems for many atheists. Their suppression or eradication of religion has meant that as a movement rather than a personal stance the term 'atheist' is often regarded with suspicion.

Atheism continues to be the official position of the governments of China, North Korea and Cuba. Here, large organizations are to be found and impressive numbers are cited. It may be politically correct to be atheist in Communist countries, but judging by the collapse of such groups and in numbers of atheists once Communism falls, the conviction may not always run deep. China is an interesting example. While officially atheist and while religious oppression is still widespread, religion in China is experiencing revival in many different forms. This could be linked to the current climate of economic change. In Cuba and North Korea however, systems have remained largely unchanged for many years, and no such revival is evident.

In former Communist states like Hungary or eastern Germany, official atheism may no longer be as powerful but much higher numbers still claim to be agnostic than in Western Europe. The impact of atheism on religious belief has been considerable, especially in states with a Protestant background. It has weakened links with formal religion, legitimated dissent from religious values and traditions, and furthered secularization faster than anywhere in Western Europe with the exception of the Netherlands. Orthodox and Roman Catholic states would appear to have a stronger hold upon people even after 70 years of Communist rule.

The proportion of people who call themselves humanists and who belong to humanist organizations is small, although a few states – the Netherlands with 25 percent and Norway with 20 percent – are obvious exceptions. The nature of these groups varies from state to state. In some countries, they have a strong scientific basis and seek to confront what they see as the illogicality of religion. In others they have a quasi-religious foundation – arising from attempts to provide a human-centred faith in the late 19th century. The American Ethical Union is one of the most clear examples. Yet others arise primarily from a concern for human wellbeing, with an emphasis on the need for moral and ethical codes based on human interests and values and not shaped by reference to a divine will or purpose. The Humanistisch Verbond Belgie (Belgian Humanist League) is an example of this.

There are many who would count themselves as agnostic, or as having no particular faith, and the number is growing. But the numbers of atheists and humanists worldwide are not sizeable and are rarely growing rapidly, except perhaps in the Netherlands, France and Norway. Beyond this, there is no doubt that the legitimation of doubt and the quest for common human values, unrelated to specific religious teachings, has had a considerable impact even on those who profess a faith.

Sources to the map:
Barrett, David B., *World Christian Encyclopedia,* Nairobi: Oxford University Press, 1982.

Acknowledgements:
Matt Cherry; Rob Tielman; British Humanist Association, London; International Humanist and Ethical Union.

14 THE MISSION

The Christian missionary movement is as strong if not stronger than it has ever been. It has 4000 missionary organizations, over 308,000 full-time career missionaries and an annual expenditure of US $9.6 billion. It is far removed from the 19th-century stereotype of the missionary, dressed in white and paddling up the Limpopo, or the notion of going to a 'heathen' country to bring about conversions.

Christianity has always been a missionary religion – the Apostle Paul was its first major missionary figure. But in the 1990s, just 1 percent of all Christian missionaries go to countries with another majority religion. Almost all go to Christian majority countries in response to requests from local churches, a principal known as 'partnership'. A massive amount of time, energy and finance is spent on 'home' mission – mission within one's own country. This is not shown on the map. Further, the total impact of foreign mission is difficult to calculate since large numbers of Christians work abroad for non-Christian organizations and engage in part-time mission. Others go out under the auspices of groups not officially described as a missionary organizations.

As well as preaching and teaching, foreign missionaries today work on agricultural schemes, housing projects, schools, hospitals, counselling programmes, computer materials, information systems, church organizing. Most missionaries work within a major denomination; or as itinerant or independent evangelists. Some use TV or radio to spread the gospel, some still travel on foot, by camel or by bicycle.

The largest numbers of missionaries still come from the traditional mission-sending countries of Western Europe and the USA. But increasingly, former 'mission field' countries are sending sizeable numbers to work abroad – sometimes back to the old, mission-sending countries themselves.

Since the collapse of Communism there has been a dramatic increase in foreign missionary activity in the new states of the former USSR and in Eastern Europe. There are over 300 US missionary groups now active in Russia. Many work with the established churches – Orthodox, Roman Catholic, Protestant and Independent but some missionary groups do not view Orthodox Christians or Roman Catholics as 'true' Christians, and have caused widespread dissent and anger. The Russian Churches are concerned that some missionaries view Russia as a blank sheet non-Christian country.

Protestant missionaries are 'invading' other areas where Orthodox or Roman Catholics have traditionally been in the majority, for example, in Central and northern Latin America. They are 'converting' Roman Catholics to the Protestant expression of Christianity – fundamentally altering the religious, social and political balance (see **31. Faith in the Future**).

Sources to the map:
AD 2000, Global Monitor, monthly newsletter, Birmingham, Alabama: New Hope; Barrett, David B., and Todd M. Johnson, eds., Our Globe and How to Reach It, Birmingham, Alabama: New Hope, 1990.

Acknowledgments:
Joseph Brankin; Conference for World Mission; National Missionary Council for England and Wales

15 A WORLDWIDE CHURCH

The Holy Catholic Apostolic and Roman Church (or the Catholic Church) is the largest single group within a major world religion. Centred on the Vatican, a self-governing city state in Rome, it claims the allegiance of 1017 million believers, and is served by 1.5 million full-time professionals (priests, nuns, monks and lay leaders). It is the only religious group with full diplomatic representation to national governments as well as to international bodies such as the UN. 141 countries have ambassadors to the Vatican, including, most recently, Kirghizia, Mongolia and Romania. Indeed the Vatican is the oldest uninterrupted diplomatic service in the world.

There is currently an overall shortage of priests to administer to the faithful. Indeed there are some traditionally staunch Roman Catholic areas, such as most of South and Central America, where the number of priests per head of population is very low. Priests tend to be reserved for 'frontier' areas, such as India or Canada, or where finance is available, such as the UK or Belgium.

John Paul II, the current Pope and head of the Catholic Church, is the 263rd successor to St Peter, the first bishop of Rome. He is the first Polish Pope in the history of the Church. Through his extensive world travels, he has had more contact with the faithful than any previous Pope. His journeys were initially undertaken to restore confidence following uncertainty and change caused by the Second Vatican Council 1962–65. Through Vatican II, the Church reorganized, and frequently liberalized, its teachings and organization. But the present Pope has resisted much of the liberalization which followed Vatican II. In his visits abroad he stresses traditional teachings, such as the ban on artificial contraception.

The 4000 employees of the Vatican, including 1000 who live in the city state, are the centre of an enormous worldwide publishing, TV and bureaucratic network. A range of specialist Congregations and Councils, comprising Vatican staff and bishops from around the world, preserve the unity of the church's teachings. The Congregation for the Doctrine of the Faith is responsible for official statements of Roman Catholic belief. Since Vatican II there has been increased emphasis on the role of the laity in local decision-making.

Local authority is exercised through the bishops of 2355 dioceses across the world. Bishops gather on a national or regional basis to decide local policies. They visit the Vatican every five years to report to the Pope. A few senior bishops are nominated to the College of Cardinals. In the early 1990s there are 155 Cardinals whose location indicate power within the Catholic Church. For example, Italy has 37 cardinals, the most in the world. The USA has 11, France 9, Brazil 7, Spain 6, Germany 5 and Argentina, Canada, India and Poland, 4 each. Some are permanently based at the Vatican, as for instance is Cardinal Etchegaray of France, who heads the Pontifical Council for Justice and Peace. The College of Cardinals is responsible for the appointment, not necessarily from amongst their own number, of a new Pope on the death of the incumbent.

Sources to the map:
Annuario Pontificio, Rome: The Vatican, 1992; Foy, Felician A. (F.O.M.) *The Catholic Almanac 1993*, Huntington, Indiana: Our Sunday Visitor, 1992; *Statistical Yearbook of the Catholic Church*, Rome: The Vatican, 1993.

Acknowledgement:
Catholic Media Office, London.

16 ON AIR

Religious broadcasting is rapidly growing within many world religions. Broadcasting transcends national boundaries and has special appeal for certain religions as a means of sending their message worldwide.

The Christians control more airwaves than any other religion. This reflects partly the traditional emphasis on 'the word' and partly the wealth of many Christian majority countries. It is enhanced by the universal role of the English language. Christian broadcasts reach every single country in the world and have 1.6 billion listeners. They are transmitted by Christian-owned and operated stations (the UK has a handful, Brazil has 1300, and the USA over a thousand) or by state-operated facilities such as the BBC World Service. The secular media may also be quite open to supporting religious broadcasting. In the UK, the BBC supports regular religious broadcasting at no charge, as do independent TV channels.

While there are scores of Protestant international radio stations, such as AWR Radio in Costa Rica, Guam, Italy and Russia, or Christus Lebt in Germany, the single Roman Catholic station, Radio Vatican, is powerful enough to reach the whole world. Sixty countries have international transmitting stations belonging to Christian organizations. Many broadcast to a region, such as the Caribbean Radio Lighthouse in Antigua or the Central American Mission in Guatemala City. International groups include Trans World Radio, which covers the world by broadcasting from Albania, Cyprus, Netherlands Antilles, Sri Lanka and Swaziland.

Some governments try to block Christian broadcasts, but cannot do so effectively. However, 32 states at least nominally ban all internal broadcasting of the Christian message.

Sources to the map:
Barrett, David B., *World Christian Encyclopedia,* Nairobi: Oxford University Press, 1982; Barrett, David B., and Todd M. Johnson, eds., *Our Globe and How to Reach It*, Birmingham, Alabama: New Hope, 1990.

17 CHRISTIAN GIVING

While never a formal part of Christian teaching, the notion of giving some regular amount of personal income to the church, if only for a favoured charity, is to be found in all branches of Christianity. There has also arisen a tradition of giving aid for overseas development, partly as a result of the 19th-century missionary movement, partly because of continuing ties between the churches of the post-colonial world.

Most mainstream Christian churches in the West are now able to use formal ecumenical church channels for overseas aid – one of the real successes of the Ecumenical Movement (see **27. The Ecumenical Movement**). Protestant churches work through the development arms of the World Council of Churches and agencies set up by national churches – such as Christian Aid in the UK. Roman Catholic churches are highly organized with central fundraising programmes in 128 countries linked through the Vatican-based Caritas International.

In some countries, funds are allocated not just from personal donations from individual Christians or local churches, but from a church tax levied by the government. In Germany and Sweden in particular, Church aid agencies benefit from these taxes (see **23. God and Mammon**). Other charities rely mainly or entirely on direct donations.

The way aid is given differs. The agencies represented on the map are typical of the broad range of mainstream aid agencies. They usually choose projects and channel funding through local churches abroad.

The agencies do not fund Christian groups alone. Most have funding criteria which forbids consideration on the basis of religious affiliation. This being said, some aid agencies, big and small, especially from conservative Protestant churches, were created specifically to fund primarily Christian groups. Such groups tend to have a stronger link between aid and evangelization.

Christian aid agencies tend to favour projects which enable recipients to achieve self-reliance – through education, practical projects and the establishment of small scale industries and welfare. While the largest Christian agencies also respond to major emergencies such as floods or famines, their efforts are mainly directed to long-term solutions of global poverty, as can be seen in the pic chart on Brot für die Welt, rather than on short-term emergency aid.

Sources to the map:
Agency yearbooks, annual reports and financial statements, 1991.

Acknowledgments:
Joseph Brankin; Derrick Knight; Barbara Stephens.

18 MUSLIM GIVING

The Five Pillars of Islam require Muslims to give or pay 'zakat', an obligatory tax on income, once a year. Zakat is leveled at a 2.5 percent minimum of personal capital wealth, after all basic necessities have been met. 'Basic necessities' are usually defined as being able to feed, clothe, house and educate those within the family. There is no legal force or administration which oversees the giving of zakat, which is left to personal honesty. It is often supplemented by further personal acts of charity. Both are given through the local mosque and are distributed locally or further afield through informal networks between mosques and Islamic organizations. A vast amount of Islamic aid is therefore untraceable or unrecorded in any accessible way.

During the 1980s, in part in response to similar Christian programmes, Muslim groups have begun to organize formal Islamic aid agencies, especially in the West where the informal networks are less strong. Aid is primarily given to Muslim states or to Muslim groups in non-Muslim states. Funds are given to develop local skills and projects such as cooperative businesses in areas of high unemployment or farming in areas of devastation. They are also given for emergencies – for example to Muslim refugees who may be fleeing from war or famine in such countries as Bosnia-Herzegovina, Somalia and the Sudan.

Only certain large agencies are shown on the map. Most Muslims still prefer to give through their own mosques and total Muslim aid channelled through Islamic agencies is, so far, not very large.

Most of the new agencies are based in the UK, although one of the largest is based in Pakistan. Its founder, Abdul Sattar Edhi, began by setting up free dispensaries in Karachi in the late 1940s, going on to develop and head a remarkable worldwide humanitarian agency.

Another form of aid, however, is given by Islamic states directly, in particular, Saudi Arabia. In this way, large sums are invested in development projects, usually in the poorer Islamic states or Islamic communities in countries such as Tanzania or Kenya. Such funds tend to be administered by Muslim religious missionaries and are usually for education, **111** health and welfare programmes.

Sources to the map:
Agency annual reports and financial statements, 1990–1992; *Q News Magazine*, London.

Acknowledgement:
Iftikhar Awan.

19 INTEREST IN MONEY

Traditional Islamic economics was dominated by an injunction in the Qur'an not to charge interest on loans of money. Through interaction with Western banking systems, however, interest charges have found their way into Islamic life. Within some Islamic states and amongst certain Muslim groups there has developed a campaign to renew Islam and the creation of a non-interest based financial system is a central plank of their programme.

Qadi Abu Bakr, a 12th-century Muslim teacher, describes usury as 'any unjust increment between the value of the goods given and the value of the goods received'. Muslims say that true trade is based on justice, that is, the exchange of equal for equal. Usurious trade is based on injustice, that is asking for more and giving less or nothing in return. Islam is not against the making of profit, but according to Islamic law, this profit can only be gained justly if the person who invests risks both success and failure. The basis of the argument against interest is that the investor takes virtually no risk and does not contribute to the exchange.

Early Judaism and Christianity also banned the charging of interest, or usury. Judaism was forced to relinquish this stand because of the precarious existence of Jews within first the Roman empire and later within various Christian countries and empires. The Christian church forbade usury during the Middle Ages. In the mid-16th century, however, Protestant Calvinist reformers gave usury official approval.

Many Muslims point out that according to the Qur'an, usury is against the Will of God. Since the Muslim world has been increasingly drawn into modern, Western banking, there have been attempts, in a number of Islamic states, to establish trading and banking facilities along Islamic principles. Such banks are trying to operate on a national level and to control other forms of banking. Some Muslim banks seek the compromise of a mixed system and provide facilities for 'normal' as well as non-usury banking.

The notion of non-interest banking is in itself difficult; it is also difficult to challenge the might of the Western banking system. Even Muslim opposition is quite widespread, on the grounds that older, pre-capitalist models of trade as found in the Qur'an are no longer appropriate to today's world. Nevertheless, attempts to develop non-usury trading are gaining popularity. Muslims keen to return to Islamic values use the debt crisis that beset many Latin American, African and Asian countries during the 1980s, as an example of the destructive impact of interest-charging banking.

Sources to the map:
Bank reports; *New Horizon*, London: Institute of Islamic Banking and Insurance, 1992.

Acknowledgements:
Iftikhar Awan; Fazlun Khalid; Swahela Siddiqui; International Association for Islamic Banks, London.

20 STATE FAIR – AND UNFAIR

State neutrality on religion, or religious tolerance, is undoubtedly gaining in worldwide support. In the West, the secularization of elites, a general increase in individualism and personal choice, and the decline in the significance of public religious practices, mean that religion is more and more seen as a matter of personal choice – of little concern to the state unless specific religious activities challenge its interests.

Both Sweden and the UK have formal state religions, yet over this century the degree of control exercised has markedly declined and a *de facto* division allowed or even encouraged. In Iceland, which has Lutheranism as the state religion, the state also recognizes and funds all other religions in the country, including the Norse religion, Asa.

The links between a religion and national identity are rooted in the past and built up over centuries. In states without a religious history, or where the state itself has been subject to change, the ties with religion are more tenuous. The map shows clearly that few 'new' nations – especially post-colonial states – have formal ties with any one religion. Where they do, such ties are usually with a pre-colonial faith, as in Pakistan or Myanmar. For the majority of 'new' African states, the concept of mature statehood assumes that religious practice is a matter of individual choice, so long as it does not endanger others or state interests.

Yet in many countries of the world, the concepts of state and religion are still intimately intertwined. In many Muslim countries, it is inconceivable that the head of state should not be a Muslim, or that the government should not follow Islamic law or attempt to rule according to Islamic principles. This stems from Islam's belief that the Qur'an and Shari'ah contain all that is necessary for the proper governing of a state.

The state may exert its authority, over religions and also its people, through either recognition or oppression. The state may also seek to protect the dogmas and certainties of its ruling group and elite. Much of the conflict between Marxist-Leninist regimes and religious communities comes from the fact that Marxism-Leninism was to all intents and purposes a belief system itself – and particularly threatened by other belief systems.

A few countries, having experienced religious conflict, seek to hold the religions in balance. Belgium, for example, recognizes five religions, and Indonesia recognizes five religious groups.

In a number of states during the 20th century, political revolutions have broken once close ties with a majority faith: between Russia and the Orthodox Church, for example, and Cambodia and Theravada Buddhism. This radical change often instigated a period of persecution, for both the majority religion and other religions too. From 1967–91, Albania, the most draconian of all Marxist-Leninist states, outlawed all religious practice.

Sources to the map:
Barrett, David B., *World Christian Encyclopedia* , Nairobi: Oxford University Press, 1982; Harvey, Peter, *An Introduction to Buddhism*, Cambridge: Cambridge University Press, 1990; Horrie, Chris and Peter Chippindale, *What is Islam?*, London: Virgin, 1991; Shaikh, Farzana, ed., *Islam and Islamic Groups*, Harlow: Longman, 1992; Szajkowski, Bogdan, ed., *New Political Parties of Eastern Europe and the Soviet Union*, Harlow: Longman, 1992.

Acknowledgement:
Mawil Izzidien.

21 LIFE AND SOUL OF THE PARTY

The relationship between religions and political parties may range from a low-key historical link with emotive connotations (as with certain Christian Democrat parties in Western Europe) to the existence of clear religious/political goals (as with the Bharatiya Janata Party, or BJP, the Hindu nationalist party of India).

The desire to separate religion and politics is largely European, arising from the need to end the long religious wars of the 16th and 17th centuries and from the growing separation of religion as an individual, private experience away from the public, secular world. This makes little sense to many people elsewhere, especially in those states where the popular faith is totally integrated with the way of life.

Most political parties with an overt religious tie (when the name of the religion, for example, is part of the name of the party) can turn to members of their affiliated faith for financial or practical assistance at elections or during a referendum. The name of a religion within the party name may also act at a subliminal level – especially among minority communities such as other religious or ethnic groups. It explains, perhaps, why German and Dutch Christian Democrat parties in Europe have chosen to maintain the term 'Christian'. In some states, such as the UK (excluding Northern Ireland) the notion of formal religious affiliations for political parties is simply unthinkable – especially as the UK becomes a more and more pluralist society.

In some countries, Catholic Italy and Spain in particular, there has been a long tradition of religious parties or parties with religious links. In Italy, the Christian Democratic Party was the main opposition to the Communist Party and in Spain, Franco relied on the Church to support him against the left. In others, the links between religion and party represent an ethnic or ideological association. In the newly-emerging democracies of central Europe, such as Hungary, the use of the term 'Christian' has anti-Communist and nationalist connotations. However, in protest against the assumed link between Christianity and conservative politics there also developed a tradition of Christian socialism, which helped form a number of Labour Parties, as in the UK or Australia. However, these parties have never overtly claimed to be Christian.

In some Islamic states, overtly religious political parties may represent a backlash after decades of Communism, as in the emerging republics of Central Asia. They may also, as in Algeria where the Islamic Salvation Front (FIS) was eventually banned in 1992, be a response to a perceived weakening of traditional values because of Western influence.

In some states, religious parties are formed in support of a religious and/or ethnic minority. The Islamic parties in Bulgaria fall into this category. Others have been formed in response to longstanding religious/political tensions, such as the Catholic and Unionist (Protestant) parties in Northern Ireland.

In other states, especially certain Muslim majority states, it is simply inconceivable that a political party could be ideologically or structurally linked to anything other than the dominant faith of the country, especially where the self-understanding of that faith is that it contains within it a unique revelation of God's laws for the running of society.

The use of religion to assert moral high ground in politics is not confined to the political parties per se. In the USA there was no formal link in the 1980s between the Republican Party and the popular, conservative, Christian movement, the Moral Majority, but the influence of such Christian groups on government decisions was considerable.

Sources to the map:
Coggins, John and D.S. Lewis, eds., *Political Parties of America and the Caribbean*, Harlow: Longman, 1992; Derbyshire, J. Denis, and Ian Derbyshire, *World Political Systems*, Edinburgh: Chambers, 1991; Hutchinson Gallup, *Info 93*, Oxford: Helicon Publishing, 1992; Lewis, D.S. and D.J. Sagar, eds., *Political Parties of Asia and the Pacific*, Harlow: Longman, 1992; Szajkowski, Bogdan, ed., *New Political Parties of Eastern Europe and the Soviet Union*, Harlow: Longman, 1992.

Acknowledgements:
Lee Kenyon; James Palmer.

22 GENERATION TO GENERATION

Every education system in the world owes its origins to religious schools and the concern for education within the major faiths. Religions have always made education a high priority: to ensure continuity of the faith, to pass on stories and beliefs, and to maintain the moral and social wellbeing of the community. Thus, many of the world's greatest universities and centres of learning have religious foundations, such as Oxford and Cambridge in the UK, Harvard in the USA and Al-Azhar University in Cairo, Egypt. Over the last hundred years or so, states have generally set out to wrest control of education away from religion. In 19th-century Germany, for example, Bismarck's nationalist goals for unification were strongly objected to by the churches. In the UK, the state's policy of acquiring control of education was part of the growing secularization of national institutions.

In some countries, religious education is a state subject, taught by qualified teachers, trained largely by the state or in accordance with its requirements. In some states, as in Sweden, its purpose is to inform about the role of religion, as central to a mature understanding of culture and society. In others, it may be part of an agreement with the majority faith, to ensure that children become familiar with the faith of the culture (as in Bahrain, a Muslim majority state and the Dominican Republic where the majority of people are Roman Catholic). In the increasingly plural societies of Western Europe (the UK is a good case in point) religious education is being broadened to include teaching not just about the majority faith but other faiths as well.

In a few countries, religious education is not a formal part of the state curriculum, but religious teachers are allowed to hold special lessons on school premises, which pupils may opt to attend or not. In India, for example, religious education is optional at the choice of parents or children, and offered out of normal school hours. This is the case even in schools still under the authority of a church.

In others, religious education is not permitted within the school curriculum. In the USA
114 this has been a historic position because of the separation of church and state in the US

constitution. In the early 1990s it is beginning to change in certain states such as California. In China religious education is not permitted because the state is officially atheist.

In the new states of the former USSR and Eastern Europe, the role of religious education is under scrutiny, as is education in general. In the early 1990s it appears that state religious education will be introduced, and that many states will follow Western Europe in not limiting it to a single faith. In Poland, debate on the role of the Roman Catholic Church in the country as a whole has centred on the form of religious education to be taught in state schools.

In Western Europe syllabusus may include the study of faiths not represented within the population at large. However teaching of Christianity, the majority faith, may still predominate in some states. In the world in general there is a broadening going on within religious education and states are tending to move away from narrow and confessional-based syllabuses. Religious education is more and more judged by educational standards relating to child development, rather than by religious standards of conversion or of nurturing children into a specific faith.

Sources to the map:
Barrett, David B., *World Christian Encyclopedia*, Nairobi: Oxford University Press, 1982; *British Journal for Religious Education*, Christian Education Movement, Derby, UK.

Acknowledgements:
Alan Brown; Clifford Payne; National Society for Religious Education, London.

23 GOD AND MAMMON

One of the ways in which religion can be effectively monitored is through financial control by the state. At its most extreme, a country may give funding to cover the bulk of the costs of the majority faith's operations. In return, the faith acts as a branch of the state, usually benignly. The Turkish government, for example, in a policy instituted soon after Turkey became a secular republic in 1923, substantially contributes to the salaries of all imams in order to gain their political neutrality.

A few other states control funding almost totally. In both Saudi Arabia and Sweden for example, the state professes one single specific religion which then becomes closely involved in the process of government. In Saudi Arabia, the practice of Islam is enforceable by law and the imams are all state officials. In Sweden, a church tax is levied on all citizens regardless of religious persuasion and Lutheran clergy are paid by the state to record all births and deaths in their area.

In traditionally Catholic countries, such as Bolivia, the Church has been seen as the third pillar of society, alongside the military and the ruling class. This has been reflected in the finances made available for clergy and for religious functions. By the early 1990s, the status and funding of the Church in many South and Central American states is being reduced. This is because the Church increasingly identifies with the poor and dispossessed, because of the rise of Marxist-influenced sections within the Church – especially those engaged in liberation theology – and because of the Church's general call for greater human rights.

In a few countries, the state seeks to maintain a balance between different religious groups and thus relies on a policy of even-handedness. In this way it hopes to ensure that all major religions are indebted to it and that none is officially favoured. Indonesia has long undertaken a careful balancing act between five major religions or religious groupings and funds them all according to their numerical strength. In Iceland, all religions are eligible for state funding, including the Norse, pre-Christian faith, Asa.

Yet other states offer substantial funding to the major faith, but ask for no specific favours in return. Germany, for example, raises a church tax to fund both Roman Catholic and Protestant evangelical Lutheran churches. Although both are expected to provide religious education teachers and they act as major charities both in Germany and overseas, the state exerts little or no control over use of the money.

Most states give very little financial help to their faiths. They may not support religion on principle (as in the case of China, Cuba, the USA and France); or because of political differences with the majority faith (as in the case of Mexico and Uruguay); or because they are relatively new states without a history of religion and state being virtually one and the same (as in the case of Zambia, Chad or Australia: all relatively recent, secular states, with no formal links to religion).

Governments will usually provide some minimal support however: via tax relief, assistance for charitable work, education, or the maintenance of historic sites. China, for example, is restoring ancient temples (see **6. Buddhism** for the many destroyed during the Cultural Revolution 1966–76) but although some are allowed to be used for religious purposes, the government prefers to see them converted to museums.

Official state religions are not necessarily funded by the state. The Church of England is the state religion of England, but receives no state funding for its own activities, other than a little help with historic buildings and for civic roles including military chaplaincies. However, the UK government does give charitable status to most religions and thus exempts them from certain taxes.

Sources to the map:
Barrett, David B., *World Christian Encyclopedia,* Nairobi: Oxford University Press, 1982; Shaikh, Farzana, ed. *Islam and Islamic Groups*, Harlow: Longman, 1992; press reports.

Acknowledgement:
Josephine Edwards.

24 ISLAMIC LAW

Islamic law is founded upon the Qur'an, seen as the infallible word of God, and upon the Hadith, the sayings, actions and silent approval of the Prophet Muhammad. God is seen as the supreme lawgiver, and his laws are deemed to be for the whole of creation, not just for human beings. The formal term, Shari'ah, means the 'clear path', indicating correct ways of behaviour covering religious, political, social, domestic and even private life.

Throughout Muslim history, issues of interpretation have arisen, necessitating debate and discussion. In arriving at a legal decision, there has to be in theory a consensus of opinion by every scholar, but in practice it tends to be by majority consensus. This is called Ijma – literally 'agreeing upon'. Shari'ah is created by the Qur'an, the Hadith and Ijma.

There are four major schools of thought within the Shari'ah, and Sunni Muslims always belong to one of these: Maliki, Shafi, Hanafi or Hanbali. They are named after the 8th and 9th-century jurists who endeavoured to clarify and set down the law. According to Sunni law, the ruler of an Islamic state is free to choose the school of his choice, just as individuals have the right to be tried according to the school of their choice. The Hanbali school is the most strict and is not found outside Saudi Arabia, where it is the official state law.

Within Shi'a Islam, which does not follow any of these Sunni schools, the 'ulama' – or council of twelve Shi'a elders – is the central political and legal institution. The judges appointed by the ulama eventually became known as ayatollahs, and formed their own courts. In Iran, the ulama is the supreme governing body and the court of appeal for the faithful. The state enforces the Shari'ah law.

While Shari'ah is binding upon all Muslims, it is officially only binding upon non-Muslims when they live in Muslim countries, and even then, only according to a special format. In states which follow Shari'ah, for example, while alcohol is forbidden to Muslims under the Shari'ah, it is permissible for non-Muslims to drink alcohol in private, and in ways that will not cause offence to Muslims.

The application of Shari'ah by Muslim majority countries differs considerably. Certain states operate a purely secular system. Turkey, for example, has a legal system based on a secular Italian model, and Shari'ah has no legal validity. Others, often as a result of colonial influence, have a hybrid system which combines secular, Western legal interpretations and structures with elements of Shari'ah. In Morocco, for example, a mixed legal system was introduced in 1961, based partly on Maliki Shari'ah laws and partly on French civil codes. Indonesia, with one of the world's largest Muslim populations, has a system based upon a secular Dutch model, and Shari'ah is only applied in the religious courts, which deal with personal and family matters.

Yet others have Shari'ah as the total legal code for the country, and strictly enforce it. Iran employs the entire Shiite version of Shari'ah. In Pakistan, although secular lower courts exist, they are supervised by Shari'ah courts which have the power to overturn any 'non-Islamic' laws and judgements.

In countries where authority is invested in the monarch, such as Oman, the United Arab Emirates and Saudi Arabia, the monarch and the Shari'ah are the only source of law.

In a number of Muslim majority countries, the Shari'ah often acts as a focus for the call for Islamic renewal. In Egypt, the Muslim Brotherhood wishes to enforce Sharl'ah as a means of reforming and renewing what it sees as a decadent society, tainted by secularism. Similar models are being voiced by radical groups in the Central Asian states of the former USSR, and in parts of north Africa, in particular Algeria. The imposition of strict Shari'ah in the Sudan has led to tensions both with Christians and tribal peoples in the south, but also with many Muslims in the north.

Sources to the map:
Horrie, Chris and Peter Chippindale, *What is Islam?* London: Virgin, 1991; Shaikh, Farzana, ed., *Islam and Islamic Groups*, Harlow: Longman, 1992.

Acknowledgement:
Mawil Izzi Dien.

25 RELIGION AT WAR

In virtually every one of the world's 480 major wars since 1700, each side has imagined itself to be exclusively on the side of God, Gott, Allah, Dieu or other names for the deity.

Religion is often so closely linked with ethnic or national identity as to be seen as inseparable from them. Thus a struggle for expressions of ethnic or national identity is experienced as a religious war. This is so of the current unrest in the Punjab, created by Sikh demands for a separate Sikh state.

Other wars are built upon a history of religious tension which now fuses with other social factors to produce violence. For example, the struggle between Armenia and Azerbaijan over the Armenian enclave of Nagorno-Karabakh in Azerbaijan is often described as a Muslim (Azerbaijan) versus Christian (Armenian) war.

Religion evokes powerful emotions and commitments. It is capable of producing believers whose faith moves them to acts of great self-sacrifice and charity. At the same time it can produce believers who feel that their faith calls them to struggle violently in what they believe to be a just cause. A recent example is the Hindu/Muslim tension in India most recently focused on Ayodhya. Here, a mosque built in the 15th century was destroyed in 1992 by militant Hindus because it is believed to have been built over the birthplace of the Hindu god Rama. While the majority of Hindus and Muslims have lived together peacefully for generations, extremists on both sides are capable of arousing violence through use of powerful religious symbols.

In many faiths, the issue of whether warfare is permissible has given rise to various theories of the just war. Such theories seek to define whether believers can ever engage in the use of violence. The usual conclusion is that violence – including warfare – is only acceptable in pursuit of a greater good. The problem, however, is who defines the greater good?

Sources to the map:
Kidron, Michael and Dan Smith, *The New State of War and Peace*, New York: Simon & Schuster, London: HarperCollins, 1991; *Ecumenical Press Service*, Geneva: World Council of Churches.

26 NEVER AGAIN?

Soon after coming to power in 1933, Hitler brought in severe restrictions on the Jewish communities of Germany. In 1940, the systematic rounding up of Jews began, and mass death camps established.

The Holocaust of the Jews under the Nazis was but the latest in a long history of pogroms and other acts of violence against the Jewish race, stretching back over four thousand years. But it was the most cold-blooded and systematic attack on Judaism, resulting in the death of six million Jews. At the same time, some ten million Ukrainian, Russian and Polish soldiers and civilians were imprisoned, of which many millions died in the camps; and over half a million Gypsies and hundreds of thousands of other groups of people such as the physically handicapped, Communists and homosexuals were also murdered in the camps.

The impact of the Nazi persecution on world Judaism goes well beyond the simple fact of so many deaths. It totally altered the geography of Judaism. First of all it virtually wiped out the cultural and historical centres of Judaism in Eastern Europe – in Poland, Lithuania and the Ukraine, and the centres of liberal even secular Judaism, such as Austria and Germany. Secondly, those who could escape went if possible to the USA, thus reinforcing the position of the USA as the country with the world's largest Jewish population – now larger than the state of Israel. Thirdly, it contributed to the creation of the state of Israel, which came into being in 1948.

In the early 1990s, attacks on the Jews continue, as does harassment of other minority groups differentiated by their way of life and beliefs. With the collapse of Communism, anti-semitism as well as general anti-immigrant and anti-Gypsy sentiments have once again been heard. Openly racist or fascist groups exist in a number of countries in Europe and attacks on people and properties belonging to ethnic or religious minorities are increasing. The question in this map's title should be a statement. Never again.

Sources to the map:
Friesel, Evyatar, *Atlas of Modern Jewish History*, Oxford: Oxford University Press, 1990; de Lange, Nicholas, *Atlas of the Jewish World*, London: Guild Publishing, 1984.

Acknowledgements:
Community Research Unit, Board of Deputies of British Jews; Institute of Jewish Affairs, London.

27 FAITH TO FAITH

The interfaith movement is not yet a major movement worldwide. At its most active, it is concentrated in countries with a high level of inter-religious dispute, such as India, the USA or South Africa, or in those where religious tolerance has at least in theory been a hallmark of the state, such as Australia or Germany. Nevertheless, the growth of interfaith work is accelerating, even if it seems to do so in fits and starts and at times lacks direction.

To many people it seems only sensible that people of religious faith – even though the faiths are different – should be able to work together. But the track record of wars and tension in the name of religion bears witness to the intensity of misunderstanding and hatred (see **25. Religion at War**). It was with this in mind that in 1893 the first significant interfaith meeting of the present era took place. At the Chicago International Exhibition of 1893, there was held a World's Parliament of Religions, to which representatives of all the major faiths came. The excitement generated by this meeting was enormous. It seemed like an idea whose time had come.

Throughout the early years of this century, interest in interfaith work increased, as did the number of bodies seeking to promote it. Some were working for a united faith, a new religious unity for humanity. Others tried to overcome the aggression and misunderstanding generated by centuries of opposition or ignorance.

The First World War dealt a severe blow to many people's hopes of a united humanity growing in wisdom. After the war, the interfaith movement slowed down. The experience of the Jewish Holocaust later shook many people within the religious communities. That Christian countries could commit such terrible actions raised the issue of anti-semitism in the Churches. The result was the rise of many Councils of Christians and Jews – pioneer organizations which have made real differences in the ways these two communities relate.

In the 1960s and 1970s, interest and contact increased between religious groups due to expanding opportunities for travel and the growth of sizeable religious minority communities in Europe, North and South America and Australasia, so interest in interfaith contact and dialogue also increased. While not always able to tackle the more turbulent religious issues, the interfaith movement has nevertheless enabled more amicable relations. In many countries it has led to more sympathetic teaching in schools about other faiths.

In some countries, a new interfaith movement has been able to help deal with social, economic or political crises. In the USA, for example, the interfaith movement only really became significant when it emerged out of the crisis of the civil rights movement, and particularly in the aftermath of the assassination of Martin Luther King in 1968. At that time, Jewish, Christian and Muslim leaders sat down to talk and save their neighbourhoods. In

Liberia, where in June 1993, civil war is still raging, the interfaith movement was formed in 1992 to enable Christian and Muslim groups to work together. In 1993, Faith Asylum Refuge (FAR) – an interfaith agency dealing with issues of refugees and migration was set up in the UK alongside other, older, social-issue orientated interfaith groups. And in former Yugoslavia, during 1992 and 1993, Muslim, Christian (both Orthodox and Roman Catholic) and Jewish groups collaborated together in an interfaith network to bring relief to those suffering in the civil war, regardless of creed.

In such contexts, the agenda of interfaith movements is established by the wider society. The faiths work together as best they can, with a common goal of reconciliation and social relief.

The environmental crisis has led to many faiths working collaboratively with each other and with environmental organizations, since no single faith can alone help to solve the fundamental issues which lie behind the abuse of nature (see **30. Down to Earth**).

In certain countries, including Chile and Algeria, the interfaith movement has been initiated by minor faith communities, such as Jews in Argentina and Christians in Algeria. These are often attempts by smaller faiths to have a voice and a more visible presence in order to be seen and heard in overwhelmingly Catholic or Islamic countries.

As part of the 1993 centenary celebrations the Parliament of the World's Religions once again convened in Chicago, as a reminder of the original vision.

Source to the map:
Clark, F., *Interfaith Directory*, New York: International Religious Foundation, 1987.

Acknowledgements:
Wesley Ariarajah; Sub-unit on Dialogue, World Council of Churches, Geneva.

28 THE ECUMENICAL MOVEMENT

The roots of the present worldwide ecumenical movement lie in the missionary experiences of the 19th century. The first major ecumenical, missionary meeting was held in 1910 in Edinburgh, Scotland. In the great vision of that meeting, all Christian Churches would be reunited in one fellowship.

Ecumenical activities were disrupted by the two wars but had gathered strength throughout the inter-war period. When the first assembly of the World Council of Churches (WCC) took place in 1948, it seemed to many as if the movement for reunion between the different branches of Christianity – especially in the Protestant world – was both at hand and inevitable.

Following the Second World War, the Church of North India was created, bringing together Anglicans, Methodists, Presbyterians and Congregationalists into one body; the United Church of Canada combined Methodists, Presbyterians and Congregationalists and a similar reunion led to the Uniting Church of Australia. However, schemes to reunite other denominations, such as the Church of England and the Methodists in the UK, failed despite a number of attempts.

The majority of significant ecumenical schemes for reunion have taken place, as the map shows, in countries where Christianity is a minority faith (as in Sri Lanka, Pakistan and Indonesia) or where both churches and state are fairly new, created during the colonial period (as in Angola, Namibia and New Zealand).

The old, historic dividing grounds of Western Europe (see **32. Foundations**) have at least become places of practical working together between old enemies. Meanwhile parts of Eastern Europe, already split between Roman Catholic, Orthodox and Uniate (Orthodox who belong to Rome) are now experiencing further divisions within these churches as well as the rise of many new Protestant churches. Ironically, by forcing the churches into Councils designed to make state control easier, atheist states such as the former USSR and North Korea have helped some of the churches to work together.

New divisions and tensions have also emerged. In Nigeria, perhaps the most significant example, some five new Christian denominations or splinter churches come into existence every week. The rise of more fundamentalist churches has also led to fragmentation, especially in areas where the Roman Catholic Church has traditionally been strongest, such as Central and northern Latin America. At the end of the 20th century, there are more Christian denominations than at the start of the century and increasing numbers of Christians are practising their faith outside the old denominations and groups.

The World Council of Churches (WCC), the main Protestant and Orthodox world body, with a membership of 400 separate denominations, is committed to unity and better relationships between the churches. Yet these 400 represent only 2 percent of the total worldwide, and only 27 percent of all Christians are in churches officially linked to them. There are ecumenical agendas within the more evangelical churches but these take a secondary place to the drive for mission.

While the Catholic Church is not a member of the World Council of Churches, it is a member of as many as 50 percent of the National Councils of Churches, along with other churches who are not members of the WCC. A much greater number of denominations is therefore involved at local or national levels.

The Councils of Churches have created ecumenical aid agencies; helped to break down barriers of mistrust; set up ecumenical laity training and clergy training and created an atmosphere in which Christians of many different backgrounds can work together. This is especially so in Latin America and African countries, where the issue of reunion is of less importance than liberation, the struggle for justice, or the fight against racism.

The role of the Orthodox Churches in ecumenism has been to work towards reunion with the monophysite Orthodox Churches of Syria, Armenia and Egypt, which split off from the bulk of Orthodoxy in 451. This is a milestone in the reunion of the churches. The Orthodox Churches have been very involved with Councils of Churches and the WCC, but they have not seriously considered unity with Roman Catholic or Protestant groups. Indeed, after the collapse of Communism, they themselves are splitting, as in Bulgaria and the Ukraine.

In the early 1990s, the primary activity of the ecumenical movement is to help the Churches to work together on common concerns rather than try to achieve a United Church.

Source for the map:
Ecumenical Press Service, Geneva: World Council of Churches.

Acknowledgements:
Martin Reardon; Churches Together In England, London.

29 EQUAL RITES

According to most criteria, all the major world religions are essentially patriarchal in their power structures, deities and formats. Within some religions there are still significant manifestations of the divine feminine (see **12. Faith in the Feminine**), but they are usually subservient – at least in official teaching – to male figures and authorities.

It may be difficult to question why it is almost exclusively men, such as the Buddha, Krishna, Jesus, Muhammad and so forth, who are the key figures in their respective faiths, but the women's movement has gone some way to focus attention on the male-dominated structures of the major religions. In the case of Christianity, this has focused upon the role of women at a sacramental and pastoral level – the role of priests and ministers. In Buddhism it has focused upon the right of women to belong to a religious order – to be members of the Sangha alongside monks. In Judaism, it is not only the role of the rabbi which has come under scrutiny but the participation of women generally in public religious life.

In theory, at least, the majority of mainstream Protestant denominations within Christianity offer complete equality to women at almost all levels of the church. All the major Protestant denominations now ordain women – although this is in debate or not yet begun in a few areas or denominations. In the Episcopal Church of the USA, the Anglican Church in New Zealand, the Methodist Church of the USA and the Lutheran churches, there are now women bishops. However, resistance is still strong and the churches may be more resistant to change than society at large.

The debate has been particularly fierce within the Church of England and its worldwide body, the Anglican Communion (including, amongst others, Episcopalians in the USA and the Anglican Church of New Zealand). While the threats of a major split have failed to materialize in all instances, the decision to ordain women has created very heated debate and may lead to small numbers leaving the church to form traditionalist churches. The pie-chart on the Anglican Communion illustrates the growth of women's ordained ministry in the churches – over 50 percent of all Anglican Communion churches now ordain women and in

1993 there are three women bishops.

The Roman Catholic Church has as yet to make any significant move on the position of women in the church and will make none under Pope John Paul II. However, groups are now being formed in a number of countries, such as Ireland, the USA and Germany to press for the ordination of women. Many theologians are in favour and have openly voiced their support. During Communist persecution of the Roman Catholic Church in former Czechoslovakia, a woman was ordained at least to deacon level, if not to full priesthood. She has now decided to remain silent, but the precedent stands. In similar circumstances, the first Anglican woman priest was ordained in China in 1944.

Due to the decline in the number of priests (see **15. A Worldwide Church**), women in many parts of the world are already playing a much greater role in parishes and in specialized ministries such as hospitals and prisons. In the Base Christian Communities, radical lay-orientated communities in the impoverished areas of South America, women play a major role. The experience, combined with the need for more priests, the rise of gender issues generally and the Czechoslovakia precedent, means that the Roman Catholic Church will probably decide in favour of women priests in the not-far-distant future.

In Russian Orthodox churches, a ceremony already exists for ordaining women as deacons – the final rung before ordination to the priesthood. Yet this has lain unused for centuries and Orthodox Church opinion is that it is an issue for the future.

The key dates on the role of women within the Protestant churches show that some churches have been ahead of society in their attitude to women's equality. The Quakers were part of that upsurge of radical thinking in the wake of the English Civil War of the 1640s. The Salvation Army gave full equality from its foundation in 1869, long before women were granted the right to vote in most countries.

In Buddhism, often under pressure from Western Buddhists, the issue of equal rights of participation at all levels by women has led to a revival of interest in women's orders. In some Buddhist countries (notably Tibet and Thailand) the order of nuns died out long ago. The question now revolves around whether any women's orders from places such as China – which has always maintained one – can restore the tradition to other countries. It is a question of continuing authority, but it has also challenged the strong patriarchal assumptions of many traditional Buddhist countries. In Thailand it is seen as being part of the whole debate about the role of women in Thai society and about the extent to which Western values can be merged with traditional Buddhist values.

In Judaism, only the Reform and Liberal wings ordain women as rabbis. Orthodox Jews are opposed. In common with many Christian women, Jewish women scholars are now engaged in extensive re-examination of the Biblical records to show how patriarchy suppressed a more equal relationship between men and women.

One aspect of this research has led to a significant debate in both Judaism and Christianity. This is the issue of whether God can be addressed as both Father (He) and Mother (She). This questioning of the assumptions of language about the nature of God has sent considerable shock waves through more traditional sections of the faiths, but has also opened up a major debate and exploration of basic notions of the Godhead.

Islam does not have the same sort of debate. For many in Islam, the women's movement as a whole is just another sign of the faltering society of the West. Islam's response has often been to claim that Islam is the true liberator of women. Muslims have questioned what liberation entails and refer to the harrassment that women suffer as a result of ambiguous sexual roles. Many Muslims point to the increase in sexual violence and to the stresses and demands made on women, and ask what sort of liberation this is. Islam sees these as signs of a disruption of a natural order ordained by God. Yet under Islamic law women have had the right to own land and property in their own right since the time of Muhammad, whereas women in the West only achieved such rights this century. However, in traditional Muslim countries, as in the West, women have been asking for greater freedom and opportunity for equal participation in society. In countries where militant Islam has recently gained strength, changes in women's clothing and behaviour away from the traditional Islamic model have been condemned and prohibited.

Acknowledgements:
Caroline Davis; Jenny Standage; Anglican Consultative Council, London; Ecumenical Press Service, World Council of Churches, Geneva; Lutheran World Federation Women's Desk, Geneva; Methodist Overseas Division, London; Movement for the Ordination of Women, London.

30 DOWN TO EARTH

In 1967 an American environmentalist, Lynn White, published a watershed article claiming that the roots of the contemporary environmental crisis lay in Judeo-Christian culture. The command in the Book of Genesis, the first book of the Bible, that humanity should have dominion over all other species, he saw as the root of our use and abuse of nature. White raised a storm of debate about the relationship between religion and the environment which continues to this day.

In 1986, the World Wide Fund for Nature International invited five major religions to Assisi, Italy, birthplace of St Francis, the Roman Catholic saint of ecology, to discuss and plan for greater religious involvement in the environmental movement. Eight religions now belong to the Network on Conservation and Religion established at Assisi: Baha'is, Buddhists, Christians, Hindus, Jains, Jews, Muslims and Sikhs.

The impetus of the Assisi meeting, plus a rise of general awareness within the faiths, means that there are now hundreds, if not thousands, of religious-directed environmental projects around the world: through the work of religious aid agencies (from the mid- to late 1980s); through education; through practical projects such as tree planting in India or Thailand, or species conservation in English churchyards.

Our map does not attempt to measure levels of environmental awareness but shows where religions have responded to environmental issues and which religions have done so. In only some states are the religions shown to be involved in environmental problems abroad as well as at home. This may be due more to differences in economic well-being than in levels of commitment.

Although the problems of the environment were first highlighted by secular environmental groups, religious involvement in the environment is undertaken from religious principles and beliefs, and not just in response to secular agendas. They may at first have been seen as 'soft' issues, but the religions are realizing that the well-being of the environment is closely connected to fundamental economic and social issues. The environmental crisis has caused a major rethinking within all faiths. The faiths are showing that they can work side by side on the environment, in a way that is unique in history – even in areas of traditional hostility such as the Lebanon and the Philippines.

In a number of wealthy countries, the religious aid agencies are now adding an environmental focus to their projects and emphasizing the link between the environment and development. This link was strongly enforced at the UNCED Earth Summit in Rio de Janeiro, in 1992.

Acknowledgements:
Joni Seager; Education Unit, World Wide Fund for Nature, UK; Network on Conservation and Religion, WWF International, Geneva.

31 FAITH IN THE FUTURE

Looking into the future, even for an atlas on religion, is a risky business. But as everyone, including big business and the military, engages in the 'art and science of futurism', so do we!

We expect the gradual spread of secularism to continue, reaching into most aspects of life, in countries as diverse as Ireland, Japan and Malaysia. In many parts of Western Europe, in Australasia and Canada, the growth of secularism will be largely at the cost of institutional Christianity as expressed in the major denominations. It will also affect minority faith communities, such as Jews, Muslims and Hindus, as constraints on the young of family ties weaken.

Although a growth of religion has been set in motion by the collapse of Communism, well-established secularism will simply continue in some states of the former USSR and Eastern Europe. In 10 to 15 years' time it may even increase as memory of the Communist system fades or its reputation is revived. In Poland, in particular, we expect an increase in secularism, in reaction to the powerful hold of the Roman Catholic Church and tensions between state and church which are already evident.

In Malaysia, a majority Muslim country, secularism will spread as a result of wider educational opportunities and the attractions of Western consumerism. The same trend can be discerned in Buddhist Japan and the Christian Philippines.

In the very areas where secularism is growing, we expect a rise in religious diversity. Interest in things spiritual, in Western Europe, Australasia and Japan, for example, is no longer confined to the historic majority faiths of these countries. With the collapse of belief in many previous religious authority structures, interest in exploring other religious models will grow. In all such states there will be some growth in New Religious Movements. More significant will be the growth of interest in major faiths other than the existing majority faith: in Western Europe and North America, in Buddhism, Hinduism and Taoism; in Malaysia, Buddhism and possibly Christianity.

We believe there will be a greater willingness to belong to small, intimate and non-hierarchical religious groups and a tendency to reject the more structured and authoritarian. This is already happening in many Christian countries, such as the USA, the UK and France. This tendency gives the traditional faiths an opportunity to re-express themselves, with the promise of regained strength.

The collapse of Communism in the USSR and Eastern Europe may be followed by changes in Cuba, North Korea and even China. For Christianity the picture is very varied. In eastern Germany there has been little increase in the number of active Christians. In Poland, Russia and Bulgaria however, the new freedoms have led to a massive revival of the churches. This revival, and the excitement it generates, could well spill over into the more jaded Western Europe. There is also a risk, certainly understood by leaders of the Russian Orthodox Church, that raised and often unrealistic expectations are being placed upon the churches by often desperate people. This may lead to disillusionment and tension.

In the emerging states of Central Asia, the fall of Communism has led to the rise of Islam. Some are looking for an Iranian-style strict Islamic state based on Shari'ah. Others are looking for a more Turkish, secular model, in which religion nevertheless has an honoured place. The outcome will be significant. Iranian-style states will increase religious tension and a missionary drive in bordering states such as Turkey, China and Russia. Turkish-style states will influence trade and commerce more than Islam.

Buddhism will continue to recover in China and other Communist or nationalist areas of Asia, and continue to spread to the West. It may be affected and changed, however, by the same factors facing Christianity and Islam in their recovery from Communism. Such changes could even be fuelled by the arrival of Western Buddhism in Asia.

A further growth area for religion is what is termed fundamentalism or conservatism a quest for assurance and certainty with regard to basic religious values and truths. This appeal for a moral, ethical and religious code which allows for little or no accommodation to anti- or non-religious standards is highly attractive to those confused and disturbed by social, political and religious change. While this return to fundamentals may be interpreted as a backwards movement, it also has revolutionary potential. This is visible in the appeal of the Islamic movements of Central Asia, the nationalist Orthodox politics of right-wing groups in Russia, and in the popularity of extreme nationalist Hinduism in India.

Fundamentalism posits perhaps the only serious challenge to the growth of rational, consumerist, secular society. Now that Communism has gone, fundamentalism is being seen by some scholars as the new opposition. In some states, it is already on the rise against Western society. Militant Muslims in Egypt and extremist Christians in South Africa represent the more disturbing and backward-looking aspects of this trend. Given the appeal of fundamentalism to most of the poor world (whether whole states as in Central Asia or poor communities such as the urban poor of Central America and the black urban poor of the USA), those preaching fundamentalism within the different religions have begun to take social and political issues seriously. The potential for the rise in fundamentalism to become a major voice of the oppressed could radically alter not just religious but political maps around the world.

Serious religious tensions, bringing war and civil war, continue to increase (see **25. Religion at War**): in Nigeria, between Muslims and Christians; in the whole of the Balkans involving Muslims and Christians; in India between Muslims and Hindus, Sikhs and Hindus; in Malaysia between indigenous peoples and the state; in Egypt, between militant Islam and the state.

The historic Christian communities of Western Asia (the Near and Middle East) will continue to emigrate as Islamic militancy grows. Highly localized expressions of ancient Christianity are now scattered over fifty to seventy different countries worldwide. Also the result of migration, the rise of small but significant Islamic communities in Europe means greater religious diversity and may lead either to greater tensions or to a more equitable relationship between Muslims and the host communities.

Christianity and Islam will continue to spread across the world, especially in Asia and Africa and largely at the expense of traditional belief. Burkina Faso is likely to become a majority Muslim country and Togo will become a majority Christian country. However, the encounter will produce more hybrid groups which fuse elements of Christianity or Islam with traditional belief.

Traditional belief may also lose ground in China. With the gradual removal of more strict Marxist-Leninist-Mao Tse Tung thought, the Chinese are not only turning back to traditional ways but also towards Christianity and a revitalized Chinese Buddhism.

All the major religions are now accessible across most of the world. As yet, most people still follow the main historic religion of their area. However, the rise of Christianity and Islam is continuing so rapidly that pluralism may in some states replace the traditional notion of a majority religion. South Korea, for example, is shifting away from its historic faith (in this case Buddhism) and into being a majority Christian state.

The indigenous Christian churches of Africa, radical forms of Judaism in the USA, new versions of Buddhism in the West – all these are arising in places far removed from their historic centres. Religion only survives when it is able to change. The rapidity of change at present, and the widespread and diverse nature of many faiths, make it difficult to say what will eventually emerge.

Source to the map:
Barrett, David B., *Cosmos, Chaos and Gospel*, Birmingham, Alabama: New Hope, 1987.

32 FOUNDATIONS

The historic roots of the world's major religions and their divisions lie in a swathe across the 'old' world: from Europe, across the Middle East, India and up into China and Japan. These are the roots of Buddhism in Nepal, north India, Tibet, South-East Asia, China and Japan; of Christianity in Europe and Western Asia; of Hinduism in India; Islam in Western Asia and North Africa; and Judaism in the Middle East and Eastern Europe. Over the centuries these have been the centres of the great faiths as well as the source of their most significant divisions, all of which still exist today.

Over the last 50 years in particular, many new and varied expressions of all the major faiths have come into being (see **10. New Religious Movements**) but so far none has captured significant worldwide support. The vast majority of those who claim allegiance to one of the major world religions would still identify themselves with the sub-divisions shown on our map.

Both Shi'a and Sunni Muslims see themselves as being more faithful to the original Islam declared by the prophet Muhammad. Yet in Islamic history, it is customary to see the move of the capital, from Medina to Kufa in 657 by the Caliph Ali to escape the control of those opposed to him, as being the turning point which led to the distinct identity of the Shi'ites. As no such turning point is usually given for Sunni Muslims, we have not recorded them on the map.

Within Christianity, the division between the Orthodox Churches and the Catholic Church is variously dated to 1054, the 8th century CE and even to 451 CE. We therefore show the Orthodox Church as having arisen from the first conversions of Greeks to the Gospel in Jerusalem in 33 CE, and the foundation of the Church in Rome to 50 CE. Dates for the foundation of certain Protestant groups accord with the first emergence of their distinct identity, in a form which has continued to today. The church in England for example, dates from c.70 CE. However, Anglicanism as something separate from the Roman Catholic Church dates from 1536, when the king replaced the Pope as head of the church.

Sources to the map:
Cross, F.L., ed., *Oxford Dictionary of the Christian Church*, Oxford: Oxford University Press, 1957; Hinnells, John, R., *Who's Who of World Religions*, London: Macmillan, 1991; de Lange, Nicholas, *Atlas of the Jewish World*, London: Guild Publishing, 1984; Snelling, John, *The Buddhist Handbook*, London: Rider, 1987.

Acknowledgements:
Elizabeth Breuilly; Mawil Izzidien.

33 HOLY CITIES

Nearly all the major religions have arisen from predominantly agricultural or small town cultures. For the faithful, the city can symbolize danger and opportunity. When a new city is created on religious principles, great hopes are placed upon it. Yet no ideal city has ever been created and cities, by their very nature, are 'impure', cosmopolitan places, full of challenging ideas and cultures.

Makkah in Saudi Arabia represents the desire for a religious city; no non-Muslim is allowed to enter Makkah and strict religious laws are enforced. Other significant ones are Salt Lake City in the USA, which was built in the 19th century as a refuge for persecuted Mormons; and Amritsar in India, built and developed in the 16th and 17th centuries, as a centre for the oppressed Sikhs.

However, most holy cities have become holy not because they were built as such, but because of events or persons associated with them. Jerusalem is holy to three faiths: to Jews because it holds the site of the Temple, the original focus of Jewish religious life, which some believe must be rebuilt if the promised Messiah is to come and end all suffering; to Christians because of Jesus, his crucifixion and resurrection; and to Muslims because of Muhammad's night journey from the Dome of the Rock, on the site of the Jewish Temple, to Heaven. In all three faiths, there is also an interesting division between the Jerusalem which is an ordinary city, complete with ordinary human failings, and the Jerusalem idealized as a holy city in both mythology and theology.

Many great holy towns and cities combine places of transcendent beauty, in an atmosphere of holiness, with the squalor of commerce, exploitation, poor food and accommodation, cheap trinkets and souvenirs, plus other 'services' for the traveller away from home. The tawdry side of holy places and those who gather for profit around them can often cause offence to both believers and non-believers alike.

In the Middle Ages, Europeans travelled widely throughout Europe and the Middle East to visit holy towns and sites. They enjoyed their pursuit of holiness, and came for many different reasons – as Chaucer's *The Canterbury Tales* makes clear. With the advent of the Protestant Reformation, pilgrimages and holy sites were considered popish and pagan and were banned in Protestant areas, especially in England. Within a few generations, secular pilgrimage routes were developed – the foundations of modern tourism. These routes still often went to holy cities – Rome and Athens or Constantinople – but did so in a spirit of adventure rather than devotion. Today, especially in smaller but popular cities such as Assisi in Italy or Katmandu in Nepal, tourist invasions by people not sharing the devotion of the faithful can create tensions with those who come to worship.

Some holy cities become a focal point of power struggles between faiths or between ethnic/religious groups. In Jerusalem, the most striking example, after centuries of conflict there is still tension between Jews, Muslims and Christians. In India in 1985, Amritsar was stormed by Indian government troops to break the power of a group calling for Sikh independence. In 1992 in Ayodhya, also in India, a mosque built on the reputed site of the Hindu god Rama's birthplace was destroyed – signalling a further outbreak of militant Hinduism. Lhasa, in Tibet, is a holy city largely destroyed during the last 50 years; China has set out to break Tibetan religious identity and brought in so many Han Chinese that they may now represent as much as 60 percent of the city's population.

Sources to the map:
Crowther, G., P.A. Raj and T. Wheeler, *India: A Travel Survival Kit*, South Yarra, Australia: Lonely Planet, 1981; Harvey, Peter, *An Introduction to Buddhism*, Cambridge, Cambridge University Press, 1990; Hinnells, John, ed., *Penguin Dictionary of Religions*, Harmondsworth: Penguin, 1984; Russell, Jeremy, *The Eight Places of Buddhist Pilgrimage*, New Delhi: Mahayana Publications, 1981; Walker, B., *Hindu World*, London: George Allen and Unwin, 1968.

Acknowledgements:
Iftikhar Awan; Rupert Gethin; Mawil Izzidien; Ranchor Prime; Aubrey Rose.

34 HOLY NATURAL

In many cultures, natural beauty has been celebrated as being in some special sense divine. Hinduism, Taoism and traditional beliefs, for instance, consider all of nature to be in some way sacred. Certain sites are especially revered. Specific deities or stories may come to be associated with them, but usually their holiness stems from their sheer awe-inspiring presence. In this map we have focused only on those sites of significance within the major world religions. It would have been impossible on the scale available to include the vast number of sites associated with traditional beliefs, although Australian aborigines and the Kikuyu of Kenya, to name just two examples, have many sacred natural sites.

Mountains are the most common natural feature to be revered as holy. Often rising dramatically from the plains, as do Mount Ararat and Mount Sinai, it is easy to see why they have been special places since ancient times. Remoteness and the hardship experienced by those who try to live on them are also a part of their appeal. This is especially true of the major holy mountains of China. Chinese poets, painters and mystics have always found mountains to have particular significance. The Chinese character for a sage or immortal combines the characters for a person and a mountain.

The Celts, both Christian and pre-Christian, found water and islands especially mystical and islands still exert special attraction for the religious mind, offering solitude and peace. They may also feature a mountain (the interaction of water and mountain has extra power) be difficult to reach, and be cut off from the easier ways of the mainland. Most holy islands are small and may become closely associated with a particular religious figure: on Patmos in the Aegean, of John the Divine; on Iona, off the coast of Scotland, of Columba; on Pu-to island, off the coast of China, of the Buddhist goddess Kuan Yin. Unlike other holy islands, the island of Shikoku is very large, yet it is wholly associated with a key religious figure, Kobo Daishi, who made a one thousand mile pilgrimage route around the island.

The flowing of rivers and the cycle of rainfall, river and evaporation may be readily linked with the cycle of life. In the Ganges, the most revered river in India, this connection is closest, since it is through the river, according to Hindu belief, that souls return to their origin and are later reborn. The use of water for washing may be associated with the act of washing away sins and evil – as, for example, the River Jordan in Israel.

Belief in sacred natural places helps to preserve our natural environment as a whole. Farming and killing are not usually allowed around holy places and, in these areas, wildlife and their habitat is especially protected. As the major faiths recognize the importance of the environment, holy natural sites are taking on a new significance. Some faiths are now looking to take the notion of sacred land out to a wider audience.

Sources for the map:
Jackson, B., *Places of Pilgrimage*, London: Geoffrey Chapman, 1989; Naquin, S. and Chun-sang Yu, eds., *Pilgrimage and Sacred Sites in China*, Berkeley, California: University of California Press, 1992; Richards, H.J., *Pilgrimage to the Holy Land*, Great Wakering, Essex: Mayhew McCrimmon, 1985.